Praise for *God's Teardr*

addiction and prostituti

"Dellenna Harper is a superhero who survived a world of brutal addiction. In *God's Teardrop*, she shares her incredible journey with love and humor as she opens her heart to expose the effects of racism, bullying, substance abuse, and prostitution on her young life. Heartwarming and uplifting, Dellenna narrates in detail how she conquered addiction and continues to flourish through devotion to family, strong faith, and by helping others grappling with substance abuse. Addiction impacts so many lives, everyone should read God's Teardrop to learn how the strength of the human spirit can surmount incredible hardship and to bring understanding to the struggle of recovery."

Susan Latoski
Retired CEO of Women's Foundation of the Genesee Valley

"Dellenna Harper has crafted an exhilaratingly honest story of the first part of her life and the roads she took to survive to the second part. Her voice is genuine as she goes from the sweetness of tadpoles in childhood to the stark reality of recovery in her adult years with all it means. Any reader who knows of addiction will gain new insights and compassion through this story of pain, purpose, and promise. Rich images that tell of cruelty and heartache are paired with hope and the powerful wonder of love. A salute to Rochester's Jennifer House."

Elizabeth Osta
Author of Jeremiah's Hunger and Saving Faith

"Dellenna's gripping story is a must-read for parents and friends trying to understand and deal with their addicted loved ones. Not only does she explain how self-hatred, guilt, and shame lead an addicted person to numb themselves from pain, she also reveals how overwhelmingly difficult it is to recover. You can send an addict to jail or treatment centers as often as you want, but if the person herself is not ready to recover, there is nothing you can do to help.

"A major insight Dellenna finally realized in her life was that she needed to get help from women. She could manipulate men. It was the women who told her the truth. That's why her stay at Jennifer House for women ex-offenders in Rochester was such a turning point in her sobriety.

"Knowing there was a happy ending helped me to endure paging through the excruciating tale of her years on dangerous streets and in frigid crack houses. I am so proud of Dellenna's inner strength and faith in God that finally proved victorious in her battle with prostitution and drugs. As she concluded, 'My worst day clean is ten times better than my best day getting high.' "

Father Jim Callan
Associate Pastor of Spiritus Christi Church, Rochester, N.Y.

"*God's Teardrop* is an amazing story of transformation and resilience. No matter who you are—but especially if you are someone who has struggled with addiction or loved someone who has—you will find yourself reflected in these pages. Dellenna Harper's raw and honest account of her road to recovery will make you cry, laugh, smile, and cheer as you accompany her on her journey. She unflinchingly gives us an inside look into her pain, process, and promise so that we too might discover the courage to face our own and get free."

Michael Boucher, LCSW-R
Co-Director of Counseling and Community Work
at St. Joseph's Neighborhood Center, Rochester, N.Y.

"Dellenna's brutally honest story of her struggle with addiction is a must read—for every woman who is struggling with addiction, for every family member of a loved one caught in the grips of addiction, for every employee, student, or community volunteer engaged in human services and criminal justice systems, for every white person seeking to understand the impact of racism on individual lives.

"I was particularly drawn to the role of Dellenna's family members in expressing their love, both tough and tender, in care and support of her. Her mom, dad, and siblings were on the journey as well, experiencing both hope and disappointment so many times, and never giving up.

"Dellenna's addiction allowed her to escape from confronting her overwhelming feelings of being judged by her peers as 'less than' because of the color of her skin and later, when having a black friend was cool, as 'more than' because of the color of her skin. Her story exposes the negative underbelly of our social norms of beauty, gender, sexuality, and race, and the devastating consequences of fear/hate-based biases and actions on individuals, families, and community.

"Dellenna's intellect is evident; she owns her choices and makes a compelling case for a path out of addiction—connecting her thinking to her feelings about herself, being willing to ask for help, and remaining open to the supports of family and community that believe in both dignity and potential of the least of us."

Jean Carroll
Sociologist, Former CEO of YWCA
of Rochester, N.Y., Social Justice Advocate

"Very few people will tell you what it is like to live in the depths of addiction. Most, even in their twelve-step meetings, will make vague references to the horrors of their memories and then slide on into a joke. In this book, Dellenna Harper tells it as it truly was, for her and sometimes for her family. The book is difficult reading in places, sometimes hard to believe for those of us who know her as the joyous and successful woman she has become.

"I have known Dellenna for more than ten years since she first sashayed into my classroom full of fire and sharp wit. Newly apprenticed to recovery and, with it, true honesty, it was what she also demanded from those around her. Her sharp eyes detected any attempt at bluff. The difficult questions that college instructors may occasionally try to fudge around—nope—no fudging allowed in Dellenna's presence. (Her challenges made me a braver and clearer teacher.)

"With that same 'no fudging allowed' honesty, Dellenna tells her story—from her upbringing to her recovery and beyond. Well, actually, she modestly omits some of her more recent successes, both career-wise and academically, but perhaps those will come in another book at another time

"In the meantime, I encourage anyone—anyone who has the guts—to read this down-to-the-bone account of what addiction can do to an intelligent and beautiful young woman, and how she climbed up from that pit and back into the land of the living to give back to others and encourage those following her path.

"In some places it can hurt to read this book. Read it anyway."

Diana Robinson, Ph.D.
One of the college instructors often challenged by the author's wit and determination to seek and speak truth.

"*God's Teardrop* is one woman's story of heaven's response to a world filled with racism, sexism, bullies, oppression, shame, guilt, and addiction. This is the life journey of a survivor who cried out from the depth of her soul.

"Dellenna takes the reader through the darkness of addiction, to the challenges of recovery, and the incredible resilience of the human spirt. What Dellenna shares is honest and inspirational and provides a pathway that others may follow."

Jim Smith
Friend and former co-worker at The Jennifer House

"I loved this book. It's written with great humility, and it's shockingly honest. How Dellenna reveals her transformation is riveting. I cried and laughed my way through this book."

Judy Simser
Founder of the Jennifer House, Rochester, N.Y.

"*God's Teardrop* is an emotional baptism that chronicles Dellenna's heartbreaking journey through the cycle of addiction. However, this is not a story of unyielding trauma; instead, it offers the connective tissue of love and hope. It illustrates the beauty of God's fulfilled promise and what happens when we are granted mercy."

Tokeya Graham
Tenured Associate English Professor
at Monroe Community College, Rochester, N.Y.

"I love the honesty and real-life experiences shared in *God's Teardrop*. By Dellenna's humility and commitment to share her story, she reaches back in hopes others may gain the strength and courage to choose life! Her beacon of light has already been an example to follow. Dellenna states: 'Self-hate is an inherent enemy. I spent years yearning to be accepted and wanting to feel a part of. I did not understand that lack of self-acceptance was my problem.' By sharing her pain of not belonging and her many other struggles with integrity, Dellenna is an inspiration. If you want some suggestions on how to choose life during despairing times, I recommend this book to you."

Julie Smith
Social Worker at The Salvation Army, Rochester, N.Y.

"The road from addiction to recovery is never easy. When the addiction is coupled with prostitution, as it so often is, the recovery can be even harder when accompanied by shame, guilt, and stigma. This book is not an easy one to read— with a narrative about life on the streets, which includes crimes, rape, and the horror of the addiction disease. But it is well worth the read. The end is inspiring, and if you are experiencing your own addiction, or work with people who are, or are missing people you love to drugs, it is a ray of hope."

Catherine Cerulli, J.D., Ph.D.
Director of the Laboratory of Interpersonal Violence and Victimization at the University of Rochester Medical Center

Also by Jane Sutter Brandt

Sutter's Sodas Satisfy: A memoir of 90 years of Sutter Drug Co.
Beloved Burlington: Featuring businesses you knew and loved

God's Teardrop

My journey of healing from addiction and prostitution

By Dellenna Harper with Jane Sutter Brandt

Wild About Words Publishing
Rochester, N.Y. | 2020

God's Teardrop: My journey of healing from addiction and prostitution
By Dellenna Harper with Jane Sutter Brandt

The content of this book is based on the memories of Dellenna Harper. In a few instances, names were changed at a person's request or where it was prudent to do so.

Library of Congress Control Number: 2020917444

Cover and book design by Sarah Crupi. Cover image from Adobe Stock Images. Back cover photo of Dellenna Harper by Doug Buckley and used with permission.

Publisher's Cataloging-In-Publication Data
(Prepared by The Donohue Group, Inc.)

Names: Harper, Dellenna, 1974- author. | Sutter Brandt, Jane, 1958- author.
Title: God's teardrop : my journey of healing from addiction and prostitution / by Dellenna Harper with Jane Sutter Brandt.
Description: Rochester, New York : Wild About Words Publishing, [2020]
Identifiers: ISBN 9781732988125 | ISBN 9781732988132 (ebook)
Subjects: LCSH: Harper, Dellenna, 1974- | Recovering addicts--United States--Biography. | African American women--United States--Biography. | Ex-prostitutes--United States--Biography. | Racism--United States. | United States--Race relations. | LCGFT: Autobiographies. | Diaries.
Classification: LCC HV5805.H337 A3 2020 (print) | LCC HV5805.H337 (ebook) | DDC 362.298092--dc23

For

Kim V. (Don't get it twisted)
You planted the seed and, because of the God in you, it grew.
May you rest in peace.

Jallanna
My feisty miracle who never gave up on me.
He heard your prayers. I love you infinity.

Paul
My hero who taught me unconditional love
and kept me alive in the hearts and memories
of family when I was missing in action.

God's Teardrop

One day, God looked over her children and saw the oppression of women. She cried a God-size teardrop that sparkled and shined. The teardrop floated to earth on a heron's wings. In the whispers of dawn, the Morning Dove's sweet song, which cuts to the heart, was heard loud and clear.

Embedded in the heavenly teardrop was a piece of the soul of our loving God on a mission to ease the burden of women who suffer. On that sunny day in June, the crystal-clear teardrop gave birth to a child Precious and Pure. A ray of Sunshine and Joy to all she would touch. A feisty fighter from day one, she prepared for her long, painful road ahead. Through her choices, she would stumble, struggle, suffer, and nearly die.

From the depth of her being, she cried to the heavens as she often asked, "Why?"

In the whispers of dawn, she would slowly learn the reason. "This will take time, like a diamond formed under pressure. The will to live is strongest in the face of death."

Fight she did, for her life, like no other. Stronger each day as the whisper from the heart of the teardrop became clearer with time. "Not only for you do you enter this battle but for all women who suffer. You will guide them along the way."

Each step she took out of darkness formed a rung on the ladder for others to climb. As outsiders watched closely, waiting for her to fall, she fought and fought and gave it her all. The answer to her heartfelt question, "Why?" was within her the entire time. Her ladder turned into a path that she became happy to share.

Today the heavenly teardrop shines a light from her eyes that sparkles and shines, for others to see as they follow her path. A light, precious and pure, love overflowing, offering healing acceptance for all who follow her path.

—Written by Jim Smith, director of Spiritus
Christi Prison Ministry, for Dellenna

Table of Contents

Prologue....................xvii
The Outsider....................1
Life spirals downward 14
Recovery on a roller coaster....................34
Don't mess with Texas 59
Minnesota repeat....................79
A prayer answered 97
From jail to the Jennifer House 109
Big steps forward....................126
Many lessons to learn 141
Helping others in recovery 154
Epilogue....................173
Acknowledgments 179
About the Authors....................183
Book group discussion questions....................185

Prologue

When I was in jail in Texas, a counselor had us write our own obituary as part of our group therapy. Then we read them out loud. I can't remember all I wrote, but it impressed the other inmates. "Wow, Dellenna, that is so good."

But the counselor didn't buy it. "Dellenna, you left out how you would die. You don't seem like the type of person to OD." She fed right into my ego.

"I know, because I can smoke or drink you and whoever else under the table."

But she persisted. "How would you die?"

I thought about that. "You know what, I would be that female that would be found in a ditch somewhere, with my panties down to my ankles, beat up and stabbed, my lighter in one hand and the *stem* in the other, in a death grip."

When you're a prostitute and you get assaulted, nobody cares. They think you deserve it. You're not a human being. I can't count how many times I've been beat up and left for dead.

But I never lost my faith when I was out on the streets. I knew I was in the wilderness. I left God. He never left me. It bugs me when people say God doesn't listen to a sinner's prayers because there have been so many times when He heard me, so many times when He saved me. So even though I was sinning at the time, I know He heard me. There's no other reason why I'm here.

1

The Outsider

When I was little, my dad moved my family out of the inner city of St. Paul, Minnesota, across the Mississippi River to Cottage Grove. We were one of the first black families there in 1979. It was like white people's land. I seldom saw another black person.

For a couple years, I was the only black girl in Crestview Elementary School. I got teased all the time about the color of my skin, the texture of my hair, and my big lips. They called me *nigger* and *jigaboo.* I was bullied and verbally assaulted. I grew up hating myself, and I hated white people because of the way they treated me. I remember in the second or third grade, the teachers tried to put me in a special reading program, for those that struggled with reading, because if you put minorities in a certain program the school district would get extra money. Because my mom and I read books together a few nights a week, we all knew my ability to read was average, if not above. So, my parents came up to the school and told them they would not be placing me in a special reading class. It was like the school was trying to hold me back for whatever reason.

My brother Paul had the opposite experience. He was about 10 years older than me and played basketball in high school. Because he was athletic and **so fine**, all the girls loved him. He was like a king at the high school, and I hated my life.

Cottage Grove was so different from St. Paul. We had lived

on Iglehart Avenue in St. Paul, and we had lots of family nearby. My dad's father and stepmother lived around the corner. My grandparents had a big dog named Bozo. I would ride Bozo. He was my protector. One time my dad went to spank me for riding my tricycle around the corner, where I wasn't supposed to go, and Bozo growled at him. My dad did not like that. "Oh no, bitch, you got to go," he said to Bozo.

I remember feeling comfortable on Iglehart Avenue. I felt like I belonged. It was a really good feeling in the neighborhood. We had an older white lady next door, and the kids across the street were all shades of color. I was little then; by the time I started kindergarten, my parents and Paul and I had moved to Cottage Grove. My parents thought we would get a better education and have a better life. And I believe that now. They weren't taking me out there to ruin my life even though, sometimes, I felt that way.

Paul and I have the same mother but different fathers; Paul lived with us. Besides me, my father has five other children. He was married before he met my mother. He had three children from that marriage: Roxanne, Eric, and Curtis. He also has two other children, Silas and Laura, by two other women. I guess you can say that "Papa Was a Rollin' Stone."

It was just the way my family was. My mother jokingly called the other women her "wife-in-laws". But my brother and sisters and I all grew up together; I'm the youngest. I'd go over to their houses and spend the night, and they would come to my house and spend the night, or stay for days at a time

My dad, Horace, was a paramedic. And my mother, Daisy, worked in telecommunications at the University of Minnesota for about fifteen years. I got a good work ethic from them. No matter what, they got up and went to work every day.

My dad was born and raised in Jefferson in east Texas. We used to drive the twenty-four hours from Minnesota to Texas every summer. I liked listening to my dad and his three brothers and cousins tell their stories of growing up, like how my Uncle Bobby Jo would get his clothes out and iron them the night before school. It took him hours to get the creases right, only for my dad to get up early before him and put on the clothes and wear them to school. My dad said my Uncle Bobby Jo would be so mad he'd chase my dad around school all day, and when they got home, they would fight.

Their interaction is so crazy, it's funny. I understand that when my dad talks shit to you, that's his way of showing he loves you. At times, he can be verbally abusive, but he doesn't really know or understand as his intentions are not mean at all. Like he'd say, "Go get me a glass a water," and I'd go get it, and he'd say, "You're good for something. We're still trying to figure out what it is." These days people would say that's cruel. I actually thought it was funny; that's how my dad was. I don't know if I was desensitized to it, but that's my dad, and I kind of have that, too. Sarcasm. Sarcasm can be a form of passive-aggressive behavior. But with my dad, his intentions weren't to put me down, that was his way of showing that he loves me. He does not know any better, that is just how he is.

My dad grew up in Texas in the '40s and '50s, when racism was really disturbing, but my mom had almost an opposite experience growing up in St. Paul. She looks white, and she's not. Because of her fair skin, her grandmother loved to take my mother and her two sisters places because they could pass for white. She experienced racism in a different manner. I remember her telling me that the black people had to sit in the balcony of the movie theater and her cousins used to always push her and her sisters downstairs with the white people. It's like you don't fit in with your family, you know, except for the older ones who like to take you places because of the color of your skin, and then you don't fit into society because even though you look like you're white, when they find out you're black, you're ostracized. On many occasions, my mother felt like she had to prove she was black.

When my dad was a young man, his father moved to St. Paul, and my dad moved there later. My dad used to hang with my mother's cousin Maceo. One time they were at a party and my mom was also there. My father was so excited to have met my mother. My mother felt the same way. My dad and mom dated for about a year or two before they were married in December 1972.

When I was in elementary school, I did not mind my mother coming to my basketball games and band concerts because she could pass for white. But I didn't want my dad there because of his darker skin color. Luckily, with him working evenings as a paramedic, it worked out. I didn't like myself; I didn't like white people; I didn't like black people. I was embarrassed by black people. I was confused.

In fifth grade I didn't do very well in school. I got an F in a couple classes because I never wanted to go to school. I made up stories so my mom wouldn't make me go to school because I got tired of the bullying. I was too scared to fight the boys. Sometimes I told my parents what was going on but not often. One time when I did tell them, we went to meet with the parents of one of the boys. We sat at their kitchen table, and my dad said, "I would appreciate if you tell your son to stop calling my daughter nigger or just don't say anything to her at all." I don't remember the parents being rude, but I know the abuse didn't stop. You know, sometimes people won't say things they want to say to your face so I can only imagine what they said after we left. Hate is taught, and if the parents are prejudiced, their kids are. After this meeting with these parents, I was even more embarrassed, so I stopped telling my dad and mom what was going on.

By then Paul had graduated from high school and had gone into the Marines. I always believed he had it easy out there because a black male in a white neighborhood who was really good at sports and somewhat handsome was praised. But as a female, I was tortured. In my mind, we had two totally different experiences. I found out later that he was also harassed because of the color of his skin.

When Paul went off to the Marines, I felt like he abandoned me, but today I know he was preparing for our future. He was my protector and he still is. He's a planner; he sacrificed back then so he can do what he wants to do today. My daughter, my parents, and me, as well as my brother's family are all benefitting because of his plan for life that he started back then.

Even though Paul was away in the Marines, he still watched over me. Here's an excerpt from a letter he sent me dated Jan. 6, 1991, when he was serving as a Marine MP in the Gulf War.

There are many things to tempt people your age. You have to be strong so none of those things affect you. Always remember to have self-respect. If you don't respect yourself, you cannot expect others to respect you…Also, believe in God and family. When no one else cares, God is always there and so is your family. We are small but strong…

If, for some reason, I don't make it home—remember I love you. Also, if I don't come back, tell everyone I accept the fact I may die and everything is ok because I'm in a better place…

I love Paul. He is and always will be my hero.

Although I felt abandoned by my brother, I did have one best friend in elementary school. Her name was Jenny Long. She was white and her family lived next door to us on Homestead Avenue in Cottage Grove. The neighborhood had fairly new homes; our house was a ranch style. Our elementary school was at the end of our block. There were lots of kids of different ages in the neighborhood, and we were the only black family for miles.

Jenny's younger brother Ryan was always annoying us. The three of us used to do everything together, and we got in trouble. We were playing "stop, drop, and roll" in the basement one time, playing with matches and lighting aprons on fire. Jenny's mother tore our behinds up for that. I wasn't her child, but she tore my behind up, too. Ryan probably told on us; he was a tattletale. Their mom was like my extended mom, so she was allowed to scold or discipline me.

One time we found these *Playboy* magazines in the basement. We called them "the boob and butt books." We were looking at them with Ryan and trying to imitate what they did. And their mom found out, and *omigod*, we were in so much trouble. We did what they did in the books. We knew it was wrong.

I did a lot of camping and other activities and fun stuff with Jenny and Ryan. Their parents were always doing something outdoors, and I was invited. I loved camping with them. My parents always had me in some kind of activity—sports, dance, church choir, which did sort of compensate for all the bullying I experienced in school.

On the weekends, my brothers and sisters and cousins would come out from the inner city and hang out in Cottage Grove with us—in white people's land. My dad fixed up six or seven bicycles so we could ride around the neighborhood. In the basement, we had Barbieland. We played with white dolls. That probably fed into me not liking myself. I had nothing that looked like me except for a couple of black Cabbage Patch dolls, which were ugly. We also roller skated in the basement, riding in circles around the furnace and the washing machine, which acted as a divider in the middle of the floor.

Out in the suburbs there were wooded areas, and we had a lot of adventures. We caught tadpoles in a pond that was down the street and around the corner. I would bring tadpoles back to the house. I thought someone was stealing my tadpoles, and my mother was finding all these frogs in the house. I didn't know tadpoles turned into frogs. We had a secret hiding spot in the woods. There were some car seats out there and we thought we were the only ones who knew about them but, of course, someone had to bring them out there.

In the summertime, some of my brothers and sisters and cousins would come to our house for a week to go to Vacation Bible School. My mom would go to work, and she always left assignments for us on sticky notes posted on the refrigerator. I hate sticky notes to this day. On the microwave there would be a note that said, "Clean me after using me" or "Cover your food when you use me." On the dishwasher there would be a sticky note saying, "Put dirty dishes in me." And all these assignments had to be done before she got home from work. She was like a **freakin'** drill sergeant. Sticky notes everywhere. I remember sitting down in the bathroom and there's a sticky note: "Flush the toilet."

On the ironing board would be another note saying, "Iron pillowcases and sheets in basket next to me." Who irons pillowcases and sheets? We did! She'd give us a dime for a pillowcase, a quarter for a sheet or a curtain. That's what she had us doing to make a little money for the store so we could buy ice cream.

One time my brother Silas and Ryan and Jenny and I had this competition where we built go-karts. Jenny and I never finished but Ryan and Silas did. They built a really cool go-kart. We had hills in our neighborhood, and the go-kart fell apart going down one, and we were laughing. It was a really good go-cart. They just didn't build it sturdy enough.

We used to travel a lot in the summer. We drove to South Dakota once to see Mount Rushmore and visit the Black Hills. We drove to Texas every year. From Minnesota to Houston is a 24-hour drive, but it took us three or four days to get down there because we had family that we visited along the way. Our summer trips to Texas were really nice, meeting all my family. My dad was a different person down there. Interacting with his family, I saw pure joy. I could tell he missed his family, and even to this day, when he goes down there, he is so happy. And his family—my family—is pretty cool, very loving and caring. I'll tell you more about that later because my dad shipped me down there and I got to spend some time with them. They were very supportive even when I was not living right.

Dad's mother, Big Momma, had a dog named Happy. I loved him. Big Momma didn't tolerate misbehavior. If my older cousins got in trouble, she would have them "hold nutch." They had to stand on one leg and put one hand on the ground, and if their leg came down, she'd hit them with the switch. She would then add some minutes onto the amount of time they had to "hold nutch". I would sit there and laugh because I was the little angel, and I didn't have to do that. She bought me a little pool for the backyard so when I was there, she let me swim in the pool. I remember I had a doll, and my cousins and I think my brother got in trouble because they cut the doll's mouth and shoved a whole bunch of grass and dirt in it. I was traumatized when they did that to my doll. That was the kind of stuff they would do to me. She beat their butts for doing that to my doll. My grandma Big Momma loved me.

I remember feeling loved while staying with her while my parents went out. She showed me pictures of my family and tell me stories of my dad. I really didn't know her that well as I only remember seeing her a few times. I do remember her hugs and feeling loved. I wish I had more memories of her.

Big Momma was a very spiritual woman. She believed in the power of God. The one thing that annoyed me was the rather lengthy prayers before meals. We would stand there at the table in front of these big country breakfasts. You could smell the homemade biscuits and the homemade syrup. The prayer would go on and on and on and on while the food got cold. I'd think, *Can't you just say what you gotta say, the Lord already knows what you are going to say, and let's sit down and eat.* But they were prayer warriors. Those are some of the same prayer warriors that prayed for me when I was lost in the world. As a result, I understand the power of prayer.

I used to love to go to church with them because I loved the music. The music has always spoken to me more than the sermon. You know when you're a kid, you're not paying attention to the sermon, but the music was always great. Even to this day, the music speaks to me. I remember when I was using, I would be standing on the corner in front of churches, and the music moved me, and I wanted to go inside, but because of the shame and guilt I felt as a result of the things I was doing, the person that I had become—I wouldn't. I could hear the congregation singing those old hymns "Down by the Riverside", "At the Cross", and my favorite "The Presence of the Lord is Here". The music is like a higher power, in a sense, especially the gospel music. It always speaks to my soul and uplifts me. There were many times I would stand on the corner prostituting myself, and I'd sing this one particular song; it was the only song I could remember at the time. "The presence of the Lord is here, and I can feel it in the atmosphere," I would sing, and then I would make up my own words and melody because I had forgotten the original song.

I guess that's from my upbringing. I was baptized Lutheran, but my mom went to the Methodist Church. My dad went to a Baptist Church, but he could never find a church like down south. He loves those old hymns "What a Friend We Have in Jesus" and "Mary Don't You Weep" sung by Aretha Franklin; and Mahalia Jackson singing "Down by The Riverside" and "His Eye is on the Sparrow". I remember waking up to my dad listening to gospel. My mom would be cooking breakfast, and you could smell it. They were God-fearing people, so I've always had God instilled in me. However, the God I serve today isn't the punishing God at all.

I remember being in a faith-based group called AWANA where I learned "The Lord is my shepherd" and prayers like that. They taught them in a fun way, and afterward you could play basketball or other games. My mother was very religious, and she did instill that in me. We were always going on church outings, camping trips with the churches, and my mom made me get in the church choir. I know I can't sing, and I would say, "Why don't you guys accept the fact that I can't sing? I don't want to sing." But I'd be in there anyway because my mom said I had to.

I always thought something was wrong with me because I didn't get the Holy Spirit like other people, running up and down the church aisle and passing out. I know today when I get the Holy Spirit, I get teary. I cry. I have an overwhelming sense of joy and gratitude inside. That's my way of getting the Holy Spirit.

Those summers spent with my relatives in Texas were very special to me because I was away from the bullying I endured in school. When I went to Oltman Junior High in Cottage Grove, I got teased there, too. I hung with the outcasts. We were the nerds; nobody wanted to be our friends. I started playing basketball. I wasn't good at it then; I did it to be a part of something, and I know those girls on the team didn't really care for me, didn't like me. But I didn't care, I wanted to belong, to feel a part of something. Plus, I liked that it was a traveling basketball team so I got to spend time with my mom in hotels.

For high school, I talked my mom into letting me go to Highland Park in St. Paul, where I had friends. Because we didn't live in St. Paul, my mother registered me using my grandmother's address right around the corner from where we used to live on Iglehart. My mom would drop me off at school every day on her way to work. After school, I'd catch the bus to my grandmother's and wait for my mom to pick me up.

I went from thinking I wasn't shit in Cottage Grove to thinking I was **the shit** at Highland. Everything that the white kids teased me about in Cottage Grove, the kids in the inner city praised me for. They praised my hair, they praised my big lips, they praised my light skin. I went from one extreme to the other. I went from being teased to being accepted, and it went to my head. It's like when you give a bully too much power. That's kind of what I did; I became the bully. But I also bullied people who bullied others, still kinda stickin' up for the underdog.

At Highland, I was always skipping class, but I always stayed on the A and B honor roll. My mom and dad were always being called to the school. I was being suspended for stupid things, like being in the hallway during class. I didn't care. I didn't want to be there anyway.

Classes were boring to me. I would rather be sitting in the hallway than be in class. I was always on school grounds, just not in class. I might not do the homework, but I would do the main stuff, such as take the test and pass with flying colors. I loved math and still do. I could have taught the math class. The math, the algebra, the trigonometry—it comes easy to me. One of my teachers told me, "Dellenna, I don't agree with the way that you do things. I had to check this over and over again because you are never in class, but you show up on the test day. I don't understand how you got a B or an

A, but I checked it three or four times." I didn't cheat. I knew being on the basketball team I had to keep my grades up, so I would show up when I needed to. My cousin and I also started a steppin' crew,

Steppin' is a form of dance with African and Caribbean roots where we produced rhythms and sounds with our feet, clapping our hands, and reciting words. I've always loved to dance, and still do. Being in the steppin' crew was another incentive to do well in school.

I was never disrespectful to the teachers, except one teacher that I told a lie on. Back then, because of the racism my dad had experienced, he said if someone calls you a nigger, those are fightin' words. And, you know, when I got in the fights out there, they would ask me what happened, and I would say, "Call my dad, because this kid called me a nigger and my dad said those are fightin' words." Those are the lessons I got at home. Don't let a white person call you a nigger. That's disrespectful, and those are fightin' words.

One time I told my dad that a teacher called us *niggers* and that's why I cursed her out. She didn't call us niggers. She told us to get out of the hallway, and I didn't, and that's why I got suspended. My dad was up there defending me for a lie I told about a teacher. I was such a brat. The teacher denied it. When my dad and I left the school, I said, "She's lying," and my dad said, "I know she's lying." I was like "yeah." I knew how to get my mom and dad behind me. I knew what to say.

My grandmother, my dad's stepmom, kind of encouraged the fighting. She was like a thug, too. She and her sister used to carry guns. I remember one time I got into a fight with a girl, and afterward I was with my boyfriend at my grandmother's house, and my grandmother asked, "Did you beat the bitch's ass?" I was like *omigod*, I had never known this about my grandmother before, so she was cool then. No one messed with her and her sister.

But now that I'm in recovery, I don't fight if someone says something ignorant or insults me. I don't get physical. First of all, I'm too little. Second, I'm getting a little old. And that's not the way I solve my problems and issues today. There's a better way.

Misinformation trickles down in the family. I don't judge my family for that. That's what they had to do. I couldn't imagine growing up in the South with the racism like my dad experienced.

In high school, I was very stuck up because I was in." I would start a lot of stuff, specifically with boys—you know when you like someone, or they like you. I talked a lot of shit to people. I'd beat them up in the hallway. I fought other girls, dark-skin girls that didn't like me because I was light-skinned. This other light-skinned chick and I would fight the boys. I would just hit them in the nuts; it was like I had a radar.

When I went home to Minnesota some years ago, I ran into someone I used to fight all the time in high school. We used to play fight. We'd be fighting because he liked me and he was like "I swear you had a radar on your hand, it never missed." He always called me a "white nigga" and I called him a "knock-kneed nigga." When you are that age and you like someone, you would be mean to them—so that's what it was. At one time I had a really big boyfriend at Highland High School named Butter. One of the bullies who was in a gang, Mechee, called me the "B" word and I said, "You see a "B", you slap a "B". So, he slapped me, and we were fighting for real. My boyfriend came around the corner and picked Mechee up and threw him through the glassed-in trophy case, and we all got suspended from school. There was a really big basketball game that night, and I couldn't play in the game because I had been in this altercation.

By the time I played guard on the basketball team at Highland, I was good with having both my parents come to games. My dad would be loud. "Take it to the hoop, Dellenna!" I loved it but I was embarrassed. "Shut up!" Everyone knew my mom and dad.

Eventually, things didn't work out for me at Highland. The administrators thought I was in a gang because when I would wear pink clothing, everything I wore would be pink, when I would wear red, everything would be red. I matched like that because that was the in thing to do. I got kicked out.

I went back out to Cottage Grove to Park High School but that didn't work out either. It was the late '80s, and there were more black kids attending the school and everyone was trying to be black. Being black was cool. Hip-hop was out, that movie *Colors* about gangs was out, rap was making the scene, so everyone was trying to be black. The white kids who had called me *nigger* and *jigaboo* now were trying to be black.

Now I was even more confused "You guys were prejudiced not even five years ago. You're the same people who was calling me *nigger*. You took my notebooks and books and tore them up and gave them back to me. I remember that, and now you want to be my damn friend. *B@$%,* please." I was being mean to them, I was. They wanted so bad to be in the black crowd. The other people I hung with didn't experience that shit in elementary school like I did. I've always had leadership qualities, I have, so I spearheaded *"F"* them, be mean to them,].We were the black mean girls being mean to the white kids. I was prejudiced because I remember the shit they did to me, how they traumatized me. Eventually I got kicked out of Park High School, and I went to Central High School. Once again, I might not have been in class, but I did the work to stay on the honor roll. I did not get suspended a lot, but I spent a lot of time in detention. Still, I graduated with honors in 1992.

Overall, I had a really good childhood compared to some. I didn't want for anything. But the self-hate that I learned from being bullied didn't end when I graduated from high school.

Self-hate is an inherent enemy. I spent years yearning to be accepted and wanting to feel a part of. I did not understand that lack of self-acceptance was my problem. In order to make me feel good about myself, I bullied others. I justified my behavior by telling myself, "I am just bullying bullies." Doing so gave me a false sense of acceptance, one that came at the cost of shaming and bullying others. I turned that self-hate outward toward others, others that I felt deserved it. The truth is nobody deserves to be treated the way I treated people. The bullying I endured birthed a self-hatred that was an invisible burden that would drag me down for years to come.

2

Life spirals downward

When I started going to Minneapolis Community College, my favorite class was "Bud 101". We had it in a van right after the first class in the morning.

I used to think that when I smoked weed, I would think more logical or be more artistic—dumb shit like that. I also used to think I'd drive better and do everything better when I was high. Those are the lies I told myself; those are some of the lies a lot of people tell themselves. I'm really good at math, and one time I took a math test when I was high and did better than when I took a test and I wasn't high. But I didn't take into consideration that I studied for the first test and I didn't study for the other. I'm telling people "it's proven—it's been my experience," that dumb stuff.

I liked the way marijuana made me feel that I didn't have a care in the world. When I smoked with the people I smoked with, I felt accepted; I belonged. Although I drank alcohol some in high school, it wasn't until after I graduated that I started smoking marijuana.

When we were in the van having Bud 101, we were so *blowed*, it was crazy. I was taking this weight training class, and I would smoke before I went in, then I'd run into the gym and do my little weight routine, and then come out of the gym and go smoke again.

It got to the point where I couldn't do anything without smoking weed, especially the drive from Cottage Grove to the community college. If I didn't have any weed, I'd be like "I'm not doing this," unless I was going to get some weed or meet someone who had weed. It was kind of like alcohol because it was so easy to get, even though it was illegal. Everyone was doing it. At least I thought everyone was doing it, but it was the people I was hanging with. I was doing it more and more with my cousins Pumpkin and Damaris and with my sister Laura.

I remember one of the first times I tried smoking weed with Laura, it burned my throat. We went to some house parties on a Thursday night, and it got shot up, and then we went to another house party on Friday night, and it got shot up, and all this time I was trying to smoke weed. On Saturday night, I said I'm just going to stay home and watch my sister's kids, and then someone shot up the apartment. I remember I was trying to smoke marijuana there. I was freaked out. I was scared. There were three big ass bullet holes in the door. They shot at the wrong apartment. Laura came home and she's calling "Dellenna!" she's calling her kids, and I'm like "I'm not hanging with you guys! The past three nights I've been shot at." But I remember that was the first time I smoked weed. I didn't smoke weed for a while after that, but when I did, I still didn't like it. For some reason, I still kept trying, and I guess practice makes perfect.

I wanted to be an accountant, because I liked numbers. I liked problem solving. But when I went to college for accounting, accounting was so boring. I realized that I could not be cooped up in an office keeping track of someone else's expenditures. I said that's not for me. I love the stars, I love astronomy, so I took that class and some other basic classes. It's no joke—when I look at my transcript—I can totally tell when my marijuana use progressed because my grades were slowly dropping.

I thought everyone was smoking weed, but everybody wasn't. Now when I hang out with my friends I went to high school with, a lot of them don't drink or smoke weed. They never did. They might have tried it, but they didn't like it.

Somewhere along the line, my choice of friends changed, and

that was when I started hanging with Pumpkin and Damaris in Minneapolis. I still had inside of me that longing to belong, back from when I was in elementary school and junior high, even though I was now praised and accepted. I liked the attention I started getting from men when I went out. I started to do things to seek attention, like being promiscuous, going to the club a lot, just being really loud, and wanting to be seen.

When I was 19, my brother Silas was shot. He wasn't in a gang but everyone in his neighborhood was in a gang. He was 21 and living over in North Minneapolis. He was pretty much cool with everyone but he saw some stuff he shouldn't have seen. He saw someone get shot.

He testified at the trial of the shooter, and two days later Silas was shot while he was riding his bicycle near North High School. I remember going to visit him at the hospital. My Aunt Norma, who happens to be Jamaican and is actually one of my dad's dearest friends, said to my mother, "Daisy, your daughter is high."

I told my mother later, "Of course, I was high. I didn't want to face that, so you know we smoked a big fat blunt on the way to the hospital."

My brother's friends were down at the hospital, and they wanted to go retaliate, and I was telling them, "Don't do that. That's not what my brother would want. If you're going to retaliate, then they're going to retaliate, and it's going to go back and forth. And then when is it going to stop? Just stop it right here."

Yeah, I was high, but I was saying, "Enough! Stop it right here!" But they weren't going to hear me. They did retaliate, and it did go back and forth for a while.

My brother was shot nine times and the bullets severed his spinal cord. He never walked again. He died Aug. 14, 1998. The doctors said it was from a heart attack; however, I had never known my brother to have any heart problems. The guy who shot him went to jail for some other stuff but he was never tried for shooting my brother.

When Silas died, my dad was devastated. I was using so I was in my own world. I know my family was devastated because everyone loved Silas. He was very brave. He was always courageous. When I was growing up, he would come to Cottage Grove and beat up my bullies. One time after he did that, a woman who worked in the school office said to me, "Please tell your brother thank you, that boy needed to learn a lesson." That's the type of person my brother Silas was. It's unfortunate his life was taken at such a young age. He didn't even get to live his life.

A lot of my brother's friends were killed. I'm not saying it's because of what happened to Silas, but there were a lot of unnecessary killings as a result of living that lifestyle. One of the friends Mar-Mar whom I had dated, was walking out of a bar and someone shot him in the head.

While I was going to the community college, I moved into an apartment with my cousin Lynn. My parents wouldn't let me move out of their house, so when they went out of town and came back, I was gone. I call Lynn my cousin but we weren't related. Our parents all grew up in the same neighborhood.

At the apartment, we smoked a lot of weed, we drank, we had a lot of guys over. One day when I came home from my job—taking photos of kids at Kmart—I saw these guys moving into my apartment complex. *Oh, they're moving into my building; oh, they're on my floor; oh, wait! That's my apartment they're moving into.*

Lynn moved four guys in without telling me. I went to high school with them, so I knew them. I told Lynn, "Hello! You have a roommate." They slept in the living room, except one slept with Lynn in her bed. But I got it worked out. When I left for work, I would have assignments on the refrigerator just like my mom did to me. When I came home, that stuff would be done, like dishes clean, refrigerator clean. Sometimes they'd be cookin' too, and I'd come home and they had weed, so we'd smoke.

If Lynn asked them to do something, they would cuss her out. But because of my feistiness, they wouldn't fix their lips to do that.

But I finally told them, "You guys have to respect Lynn. If she asks you to do something, you have to do it. It's her house too." She'd be crying, and I was like "You're the dumb ass that moved them in."

Around that time, I got pregnant. I took a home test that said I was pregnant, but when I went to the doctor, they said I wasn't pregnant. I didn't know I was pregnant until I was in my fifth or sixth month. The timeline was all messed up. I think it was because I was still taking birth control pills, still having my period, and still smoking weed throughout my pregnancy. And I was smaller than a normal pregnancy. I thought about getting an abortion, but it was too late, I was too far along in my pregnancy. I am glad I didn't.

I had had an abortion when I was 16 years old. I know today that abortions are not a form of birth control and that whether you decide to keep a child or abort the child, your life will never be the same—not as you knew it was before the pregnancy. Both decisions leave you with feelings for the rest of your life.

When I found out I was pregnant, I stopped smoking cigarettes, not because I was pregnant but because I did not like the taste. I also stopped drinking, but I did not stop smoking weed. I couldn't stop, even if I wanted to.

I do not know who the father of my daughter is because I was promiscuous. I had two guys take a paternity test and neither is the father.

When Lynn found out I was pregnant, she just judged me. Come to find out, she was pregnant, too. Lynn ended up moving out, and our friend Chanel moved in. Chanel and her boyfriend, Mike, had been at the apartment a lot.

One night in late April 1994, I was having contractions, so I called the doctor and was told to wait until my appointment the next day. I went to my appointment and the nurse told me that I was dilated to seven and to go straight to the hospital; she specifically told me not to go home. I left the doctor's office, went home, smoked a blunt while I packed a bag, then told Chanel that the baby was coming, and she needed to take me to the hospital. She was all over the place. While driving to the hospital I asked if she was OK and if she needed me to drive, and she said she was fine. I only asked her because she passed the exit to the hospital, she was so nervous.

When we finally made it to the hospital, the nurses told me I had to walk, so I walked and I walked and I walked. A female minister from my church was telling me to breathe and then the doctor was telling me to push and I heard this screaming and I saw this pale yellow little baby, my baby, and at that moment I fell in love. Newborns look ugly to me and my baby was no different. She looked like a little yellow troll. That is really all I remember. I later saw pictures my mom took of everything else that I don't remember.

My mom was so happy, she was showing pictures to everyone, pictures of Jallanna's head coming out. I was like "Mom, you cannot show everyone those pictures. That is my vagina in the picture, you know." She didn't care, she was just so happy. It looked like a bloody massacre in the photos. But all she saw was her grandbaby's head coming into the world. Never mind the fact that my legs were cocked up in stirrups, never mind all the blood, never mind my private parts in the picture—all that mattered was her grandbaby was entering the world.

Jallanna was a blessing to my life. She was and still is my miracle. She gives me hope. When she was born, none of the names I had picked out seemed to fit her. We called her all kinds of names for the first few weeks. My cousin Cordell was over at the apartment one night and he said, "Name her Jallanna." Dellenna and Jallanna. I liked it. So my cousin is the one who named her.

After I had Jallanna, out of all the messed-up decisions I made, I did do a good thing. I chose Chanel and Mike as Jallanna's godparents, and Chanel has been an awesome godmom, absolutely wonderful.

After Jallanna was born, I was messin' with this guy named Mario. He and his cousin Leroyce lived in the other building. One time they were snortin' cocaine and I tried it. I didn't like the tingly feeling in the back of my throat. Mario didn't want me to do it at first, but you can't tell me no. So I tried it. And even though I didn't like it, I came back and tried it again.

So then for a while, all I was doing was snorting. It was easily accessible because Mario was selling it. He started staying over at our apartment. By this time, Chanel was telling me, "You're trippin', 'D'." I was kind of losing it. I remember one time, I found a stash and I thought it was cocaine, but it was heroin. I didn't know the difference, so I snorted it, and I laid in the bed, and I said to myself, "I don't think that was cocaine." I did not like the way that shit made me feel. I prefer uppers, not downers.

But I was trying to get out of self. I was not OK with self. When I say I was not OK with self, I am really talking about a lack of self-acceptance. I still struggled with self-hate, wanting to belong somewhere and feeling like I don't belong anywhere. I also struggled with low self-worth and lack of confidence. I wanted to be anybody but who I was. Looking back, I probably had post-partum depression, too. I felt different when I was under the influence of drugs. I felt confident and like I was a part of something. I was wanting to feel any way other than how I was feeling. I know today that those feelings were false—a false sense of confidence and a false sense of belonging. So even though I didn't like the heroin high, I was still snortin' it. Anything to get me out of self.

I remember just snortin' it and snortin' it and wantin' that rush because then you're chasin' that first one. You never get that first rush again. You're just chasin' it, and that's what I was trying to get. Now at the time, I did not realize that you get dope sick when you have a heroin habit and you don't have any heroin. I was so sick I couldn't even take care of my baby when I didn't have any heroin. I did go to the doctor, and I was honest with him and he said that it was the heroin that was causing me to be sick. It wasn't a **bad** withdrawal because I didn't have much of a habit but it was bad enough. My body was sore, my nose was running. I was throwing up, I had body aches, and I thought I had the flu. I can only imagine what it would have been like if I'd snorted the heroin for a couple more days. After that I decided I would just stick with the cocaine, or so I thought.

When I was smoking only weed, I used to talk about people who smoked crack, calling them crackheads. I would talk about them like they were a dog, and never once did I know that I would become a crackhead *ho*. One time I was at my apartment with this girl that I went to high school with, and she had a crack pipe.

"Let me try that," I told her.

"You don't want to try this. You know, I looked up to you in high school. You were popular. You're good, and you don't want to do this."

"Yes, I do."

She wouldn't let me try it. But her dad came over to the apartment and offered to give me oral sex for drugs. And I was like *OK, at least I'm not giving the sex*, and I ended up hitting the pipe that night with him. Before that I was smoking cocaine out of a soda can, which is less potent than smoking from a glass or metal pipe. This is how crazy and sick the drug lifestyle is. When they say that with the first hit, you're addicted, that is so true. You're chasing that first high that you never feel again unless you stop smoking for a couple of days. It's not physically addictive like the heroin; it's psychologically addictive, you just want more. And you'll do anything to get it. That was the beginning of the end.

I was still with Mario, and he was cheatin' on me. I was smoking crack out of a can and Mario didn't know about it. And I was smoking it with a white guy in my apartment, and he was telling me that Mario was at a hotel. I drove to the hotel, and I found out what room he was in, and I got the maid to open the door. He and a girl were laying in the bed, and boy, was I making a scene! I was cussing and hitting him and threatening her.

I started to leave in my car and Mario came out of the hotel. If I hadn't had a stick shift, I would probably be in jail for vehicular manslaughter because I tried to run him over. He ran up the hood of the car, over the top and down the back. That's the only reason

I didn't hit his ass. I laugh at that today. He later passed away of an overdose in about 2014. He was clean for a while, and we stayed in touch. He'd say, "Remember when you tried to hit me with your crazy ass, you tried to run me over," and I'd tell him, "I would have, too."

I hooked up with my cousin Cordell; he supplied me with drugs to sell for him. One time after I got all this money from dealing, I got high with this girl. I had been up for about a week, so I fell asleep. We call those types of sleep "crack comas" when you're sleeping so hard after being up for days or weeks at a time. I had all this money on me that I owed Gerald, and she stole it. Shit like that was happening, and by this time I had very little furniture in my apartment. Chanel had gotten tired of my shit; she took her stuff and moved out. I sold the kitchen table to get some cash and was using with the people I had over there. Eventually I lost the apartment because I wasn't paying the rent. I moved in with my mom and dad.

Shortly before I moved out, I think Chanel was on the phone with my mom saying, "Dellenna is trippin' over there, you got to do something. Get Jallanna out. Relatives lined up to come and get Jallanna for the weekend. My daughter was the first grandbaby on my mom's side of the family, the first cousin, so she was like the "suitcase child". When she was gone, that gave me an excuse to party.

To get my parents off my back after I moved in with them, I went to a treatment center at a hospital in St. Paul. While I was there, I would collect money from the other patients, and I would sneak out past the nurses, past the guards, go downstairs, and get out and go get drugs, then sneak back in. We'd all be getting high. The nurses would take blood samples every morning, and they're wondering why our levels weren't getting low, not realizing we were using in the facility. My cousin would come to visit and bring me drugs, too.

I had a soda can I was smoking cocaine out of. I'd get ashes from the smoking room and put them on the can. Then I would put a dent in the can and use a safety pin or other sharp object to poke holes in the dented part. Then I'd put some ashes on it from a cigarette, put the crack on the ashes, poke a hole on the side to use as a carburetor, then light the crack or marijuana, while covering the hole on the side. As I sucked the air out of the can, I'd take my finger off the hole and inhale the crack or weed through the top of the can. You can make a pipe out of pretty much anything.

This treatment center had a twelve-step program. This was the first time I heard about any kind of twelve-step program. The center had evening programming that included a variety of recovery-oriented presentations. One particular presentation involved a man who told us how he had sold all the shit out of his house when he was using. I couldn't identify with that, not yet anyway. I thought, *He's crazy* because I was only looking at the differences between him and me, not the similarities. His wife was there, and I wondered how the hell could she be with him. She's a dumb ass. I was totally judging him because, in my mind, I was still employable—I had a job. But I hadn't experienced a bottom such as his yet. I can't remember if I completed that program, but I think I had to leave after fourteen days because my insurance ran out. Needless to say when I got out, my disease was progressing. I didn't think of losing my apartment and having to move back in with my mom and dad as homelessness: "You lost your housing 'cuz of drugs." Today I recognize that I did. At that time, I thought I wasn't homeless because my family supported me.

After the treatment center, I lived with my mom and dad. I was drinking alcohol but not smoking crack or weed. My mom and dad asked me, "Should you be drinking?" and I was like "Yeah, as long as I'm not smokin' crack. Crack was my drug of choice, not alcohol." I was sittin' at home all day with Jallanna while my mom and dad were at work. I put a real bad dent in my dad's alcohol stash. I put water in the bottle so he wouldn't notice. I think it got a little too watery and he got suspicious.

I was hanging with my cousins and started smoking weed again, and my mom and dad found out. Eventually the alcohol and weed led me back to smoking crack. One Sunday I went to church with my mom and Jallanna. I told my mom I was going to go to the store, but I actually went to go cop drugs from a woman who lived right around the corner. I was getting high in my mom's van outside of the church and decided to continue to smoke in the bathroom of the church.

Yeah, I know, great idea! I was going back and forth from the bathroom to the sanctuary. When I went up to the sanctuary the last time, the sermon had started, and I noticed my mom was gone. I asked Jallanna, "Where's Grandma at?" and she didn't know. I walked downstairs to the church office, and my mom was on the phone. She told me she was talking to my aunt, but she really was on the phone with my brother Paul, who was a police officer.

She called my brother to come arrest me! I was listening to the sermon, and the deacon tapped me on the shoulder. There was my brother is in the back of church, swingin' handcuffs. He arrested me in front of everybody. I'm thinking, *Is this even legal? Can family arrest family?* My mom is standing in the hallway yelling "The little bitch was getting high in the bathroom." She was so fed up.

I said, "Mom, we're in church, stop cursing!" I was embarrassed, not for smoking in the bathroom but because my brother is arresting me, my mom's cursing in the damn church—they're going to hell! I was embarrassed for all the wrong reasons. My brother put me in his patrol car. He had this big gun between us. He asked me, "Who sold you the drugs?" I didn't tell him because she's an older lady. I told him some dude on the corner named Black. I was so high I wasn't even scared. I was fearless. Paul didn't take me to jail; he just drove me around and gave me a good scare. He later told me that he almost shot the dude he thought had sold me the drugs.

When I got home, my mom told me, "I need you to be gone when I get back." I was pleading with my dad, trying to get him to let me stay. He was talking to my mom on the phone, and I heard her say, "I'm not coming home until that little bitch is gone."

My mom doesn't usually curse. She's a very meek and humble

woman, but she was just done. She had had enough. She was tired of watching me kill myself. She took Jallanna and my niece and went somewhere.

I sat on my dad's lap, and I was crying and he said, "Dellenna, we can't go on like this." He was crying, too, and he said, "You come from a long line of strong black women, so I know you have it in you to beat this thing," and he was naming them, like my grandmother Big Mama and his Aunt Nanny Vye and my other grandma who we call Gommy. "You know, you can beat this thing, you just gotta try." I'm daddy's little girl and he was always on my side. But he was not gonna let me stay. I don't know where I went from there. I think my mom or my dad dropped me off somewhere. I was homeless pretty much by choice because I had other family members where I could stay. But because of my embarrassment, my guilt, my shame, I wouldn't do it. I wouldn't stay with them.

I'd see my sisters sometimes when I was out standing on the corner. Laura would drive right past me and just turn her head, like she didn't see me. I believe she was embarrassed and sad for me. But if my sister Roxanne drove by, she would stop. I would run from her and she would chase me and snatch me up and take me to her house and feed me. But I would always leave.

After some time went by, I moved back home. My parents, Jallanna, and I went to a family reunion on my mom's side in Missouri, and there I met my cousin Tanisha. We connected because we were both crazy, like fun crazy, and we both just happen to smoke weed. I found out that Tanisha lived in St. Paul. We started hanging out and she eventually came to live with my mom and dad and me; she stayed in a smaller room in the basement. We were smokin' weed and drinkin' and going out, but my mom was a lot more content with me doing that, than seeing how I had been on the crack.

We got jobs at a telemarketing place. We did a lot together. We went bowling. We were always at the bar at Mall of America playing pool; we thought we were pool sharks. We played for money and we were somewhat good. We knew who to bet, and we also knew how to get a guy's head out of the game—you know, with the clothes we were wearing, bending over in front of them.

One time we went home with these random guys. I remember being in a hot tub in 30-degree weather outside in Minnesota. I had sex with one of the guys and I didn't even remember it the next day. I had blacked out. Tanisha told me, "You were trippin'." When I drink Tanqueray gin, I always black out.

There were these guys from Detroit, big tricks. They liked to spend money and we didn't mind spending their money. We would go shopping. The guy I was messin' with was named "Money". They were drug dealers, not the on-the-corner kind of drug dealers, but big drug dealers. That's why a lot of people from St. Louis, Chicago, and Detroit came to Minnesota because there was a lot of money to be made selling drugs.

"Money" was doing powder cocaine. He would come get me sometimes, and we would snort some powder. We would go shopping with them. One time they picked us up from work, and they were being assholes, and I guess they paid like $50 for this blunt that they were smoking but they wouldn't let us have any, so I said, "If we can't smoke, ain't nobody smoking," and I snatched the blunt out of "Money's" mouth and threw it out of the window while we were driving on the freeway. And he took my hat and threw it out the window. I said, "That blunt cost more than that hat." I thought that was so funny.

Tanisha and I were just crazy. Tanisha used to be so mean. She could be nice, but if you disrespected her, then it was on. My boyfriend at the time, Malo, called her "Fire". Everywhere she went, she would always get in an argument with someone. Tanisha didn't fight that much; she was more of a shit-talker like me. Except one time we were at a Taco Bell in St. Paul, and this lady was taking our order and just being rude. Tanisha said, "Bitch, I will come behind the counter and whup your ass back to Somalia." All of a sudden Tanisha was over the counter and about to beat her ass. I had to grab Tanisha and drag her out of there.

Malo played in a band called Tribe of Millions. They were really popular. He's a genius on the guitar. He even did some work with Prince at some point. I went to the Minnesota Music Awards where Malo won a couple of awards. Every time he had a show, Tanisha and I would get in free and drink free all night. One of the band members liked her, but Tanisha cussed him out. That is exactly why "Fire" was her nickname.

Malo didn't smoke or drink. Some of his family did, but he chose not to do it because he saw what drugs did to them. His uncle was a heroin addict. His band members drank and smoked weed. I used to get high with them all the time. It didn't bother Malo at all. He was the manager. He's seen me at my worst, and he's seen me at my best. I'd go to his house after using for days and he'd play the guitar and sing to me. I would just fall asleep I was so tired.

When I was about 24 and Jallanna was about 4 years old, around Christmas time, I asked Malo if he would give me some money so I could buy her some gifts, but actually I was trying to get high. Instead of giving me the money, he went and bought the gifts. I think he knew what was going to happen to that money if he gave it to me.

Tanisha and I were working at a phone service company in St. Paul at the time. I started out in telemarketing selling the phone service. I did not find out until later that we were changing people's phone service and charging them more money. Then Tanisha and I moved into customer service where we got the calls from irate people, because we had slammed/switched their phone service. We would calm them down by switching their service back to the original provider. The callers could be extremely rude, rightly so, but after a while I was being rude back, although I knew what we were doing was wrong.

I hooked up with a woman who also worked there, and we started smoking crack together. Things started to unravel with all the secrets I was keeping. I'd be missing for days; I'd be over at this woman's house getting high. Tanisha was like "What the fuck, what's going on?"

By this time, my behavior came between me and Tanisha because I was lying and telling people she was smoking crack, to get the focus off me. But she wasn't. One day at work after we got paid, I stole some money out of Tanisha's purse when she went to lunch, and then I left. She talked to some guy who worked there, and she figured out it was me who took the money. That's when we fell out. She still stayed at my house but we were very distant. I had put a big wedge between us with all the lies I had told. She told my mom and dad that I was smoking crack, and I was telling them that she was smoking crack. She was not smoking crack, I was. Needless to say, she later moved out.

I got fired from that job, and they gave me a check for $5,000, and that shit was gone just like that. The check was probably hush-hush money because they knew what they were doing was wrong.

I started to take my parents' cars again, and I would go get drugs and smoke all night. When I ran out of money, I would hook up with drug dealers and prostitute myself for drugs. This was when I learned that I could get drugs by using my body. Basically I was doing a lot of sucking and fucking. That was my means of getting drugs.

I remember my mother saying, "Dellenna, you are losing your fucking mind." My mom doesn't usually cuss like that. But in a sense, she was right; she was absolutely right.

I wasn't just stealing my parents' cars; I was stealing their money. I remember stealing the mortgage money and pretending I didn't and helping my mom look for it. Then when she went to bed, I took her van and went to go use in the city. I would have the van back in the driveway by the time her alarm went off. I would come in the back door and go right downstairs to my bedroom in the basement and play sleep after I'd been up all night. Jallanna slept in her own room, or sometimes with my mom and dad, or sometimes with me.

One time I took Jallanna with me to go cop. That's one of the stupidest things I've done. When I got to the place, I left her in the van sleeping, went upstairs in this house, got some drugs, came back down—and she was still sleeping. I had a flat tire, so I went to this Holiday gas station downtown and I got a police officer, who happened to be there, to change the tire. While he did that, I was in the back seat of the van smoking crack.

Life was just crazy. After my parents went to sleep, I would crawl on my knees into their bedroom, like I was in combat or something, trying to get to my mom's purse. She kept it under her pillow. My parents were sleeping like victims or hostages in their own house, hiding shit from me, all kinds of crazy stuff. I tried to sell my mom's accordion, but no one would buy it.

By that time, I had stopped working except for a little side job here and there. I worked at a pool hall, which was also a restaurant and a bar in Galtier Plaza in St. Paul. That's where I got my drugs. One of my other brothers was living with us then. He and his girlfriend and I were all using. They would meet me at the plaza, and we'd get high. Eventually I didn't want to smoke weed; it was all about smoking crack. When I wasn't smoking, I was drinking at the bar, and I wasn't supposed to be drinking when I was working, but I needed **something,** and the weed just wasn't getting it anymore.

This is what I wrote in a journal in 1999 while I was in a treatment center:

My family and friends objected to my dishonesty. My family objected to the amount of time spent with my daughter and them, which was none. My mom would tell me I look like hell when I came in high. She would drag me to the mirror, crying, saying look at you, just look at u, look what you are doing to yourself. I would tell her I look fine, what's wrong with me. I saw a picture I took when I was high. I remember I thought I looked cute that day but looking at the picture (now) I looked like the walking dead.

Around this time my family did an intervention. My mom lied to me and told me she was taking me somewhere. I agreed to go. She had this big ass hockey duffle bag and I asked her what's in the bag, and she told me another lie. We get to this center and I see my Aunt

Rita, my Uncle Walter, my Dad, my Aunt Peggy, and I'm like "Oh shit". It was like that TV show *Intervention.* Everyone went around the circle and told about how my behavior affected them and how concerned they were. Just when I was thinking *OK, they're done*, my brother Paul walked in. I was like *Oh fuck.* He was still a police officer at the time, and he lost it, talking to me and crying.

Then they dumped the duffle bag out and there was all my paraphernalia, all my lighters and cans I used smoking the crack. I would get high in my room in the basement, and leave and go do something, and when I came back, my shit was gone. I was thinkin' I'm losin' my mind. My mom had been going down into my room collecting evidence.

I couldn't even lie. I felt so naked; I felt exposed. I felt like getting up and running. I said, "OK, I'll go to treatment, whatever." They all left, and I talked to the counselor. I went outside, I found a drug dealer, I came back in, I got a soda out of the machine, I went into the bathroom, dumped the soda down the toilet, made the can into a pipe, and got high. I didn't like the way I was feeling. I'd do anything to stop the way I was feeling.

In 1999, I wrote about that day in the same journal. *I was mad at my family for coming and really angry with my mom. I was relieved Paul was not there but when he came in late, I just knew it was over with. I expected him to preach to me. He cried and talked to me and I cried too. After the intervention was over, I was so hurt I went and medicated the pain. That's all I knew. I felt hurt when talking about a situation involving my daughter and my addiction.*

That intervention left me feeling exposed, vulnerable, embarrassed, shameful, and guilty. I was so sad and empty for hurting my family, angry at myself and them for setting me up for this intervention. I did not have the ability, at that time, to just sit with those feelings. I did not want to feel those feelings. I did what I normally do, and I numbed myself by using. Interventions are a good tool when people are ready to change. I was not ready. I may have hit my bottom at that time, but my bottom had a trap door. I was not done. Although I went to treatment, I dug a deeper bottom and continued to use. One thing people do not understand is that if an addict is not ready or willing to stop, there is nothing any one can do to stop them. You can lock them up, pray over them, beat them, send them away to the mountains or even the moon. But if they are not ready, they will not stop.

After the treatment at this center, I moved to a halfway house on University in St. Paul. It was a really nice house, and I followed the rules for a while. I had a sponsor, and I was going to twelve-step meetings, but I was still hanging with some people that I had no business hanging with. Mind you, I was using in the facility. I used in every facility back then. I can't count how many treatment centers I've been in; it's hard to keep them straight.

Despite my addiction, I never had a problem getting a job. I worked with a realtor named Ishmael that my brother Silas knew. I helped with behind-the-scenes stuff when he sold a house. He also owned some rental properties. I would call the renters and say the rent was due. I was brutal with them, too, with his permission. But I was using drugs more and more. I'd get high in the bathroom there. I would call friends and ask them to come get me at lunch time to drive me down the street to where I could buy drugs. One time I called a friend of my brother Silas who I used to date. I had him take me down there to cop and take me back to work. He didn't know what he was doing. He just wanted to see me and see how I was doing. I could have put his life in jeopardy.

I don't think Ishmael, at the beginning, really knew what was going on. He tried to help me. He told me "You gotta get your stuff together." But I'd be in the bathroom getting high. I eventually got let go from there, too.

While I was still working there, I was in an outpatient program and living with my parents in Cottage Grove. I met this guy, Doug, who was in the program dealing with his alcoholism. We did the outpatient dating thing. His parents were so rich. They had a big ass house outside of Cottage Grove way back up in the woods with this hot tub outside, so we were always in 30-degree weather chillin' in the hot tub. He had been married but was divorced. He was in the process of getting custody of his two daughters. Sometimes Jallanna and I would do things with them.

I felt uncomfortable around his parents because of my past, doing drugs and stuff like that, plus the fact that I'm black and he's white. He kept telling me, "My parents are cool; they don't care. Hell, look at me, I'm in the same outpatient program you are." But at the time I was consumed with guilt and shame. I felt less than but they never made me feel less than. They were really nice; they went above and beyond to make me feel welcome. My shame and guilt would not allow me to feel welcome or accepted.

Doug was my first white boyfriend. I never thought I would date a white boy after all the bullying I had experienced in elementary school and junior high, but Doug was cool. My mom and dad were fine with our dating. My dad said, "I don't care who you mess with as long as they treat you right."

I was at Doug's house when I found out Silas had died. He was only 26. I was devastated. I felt guilty because I hadn't visited Silas in a couple of months. Because of my drug use, I had not been there for him like he was for me. He was my protector when I was young and when he needed me, I didn't show up. I always thought about going to see him, but I never made it there. I felt lost and confused because my brother was gone. I didn't even get to say goodbye. I didn't get to tell him how much I love him. I took for granted that he would always be here even in his paralyzed condition. I was so selfish, only thinking of myself. I felt so guilty. All of this was just the perfect excuse to get high and go hard at getting high. At the funeral, I was high out of my mind. I barely remember it. I do, however, remember standing next to my brother's casket, looking down at his dead body, while I was also dead inside. I was like a zombie, the drugs were not only killing me, but they were changing me.

When people use drugs, their personalities change. The drugs just consumed me. I never thought about how the rest of my family was feeling because of my own self-centeredness. I didn't give a fuck about anybody, not even my daughter or myself. Anything that got in the way of me getting high had to go.

After the funeral, my parents had had enough. They thought that getting me out of Minnesota would help. They wanted me to go to Texas to a halfway house where my cousin, who was in recovery, worked. They did not understand that no matter where I went, I was taking my thinking with me. Because I was not ready to change, nothing but my external environment changed. They thought my cousin could save me. What they did not realize was that no one could save me. I had to be the one to save me, and I wasn't ready to save myself.

3

Recovery on a roller coaster

My cousin, Gloria, worked at a halfway house called HALT in Houston. My parents decided to ship me down there after my brother's funeral where I was high as hell. They thought my cousin could save me.

We drove down there—my daughter, who was about 4 at the time, my mom, and my dad. HALT stands for Hungry, Angry, Lonely, and Tired. It was a nice place. I learned a lot about the disease of addiction and picked up some life coping skills. We did a lot of writing assignments there, too.

On Dec. 24, 1998, I wrote an essay called "Championing Our Inner Child." The essay began:

Championing our inner child is a form of correcting or parenting our inner child. The inner child is terrified of abandonment. We need to re-parent the child and find ways to nurture ourselves effectively.

Later in the essay, I wrote about trust, addictive behavior, and acceptance.

With trust, it has to be proven to me first. I don't trust people right away. They have to prove to me that they are trustworthy. With addictive behavior, I do have an addictive personality. I tend to take things to the limit. I do know I am drawn to whatever addiction to compensate for the emptiness I feel. I think the emptiness is a lack of spirituality for me. I'm sure it's something else but I haven't figured it out yet. I guess that's something I can work on while I'm here. And the last one is acceptance. I love attention. All the attention in the world is not enough. I am working on that. I will go to great lengths to be accepted.

I copied this poem in January when I was in HALT. I don't know who the author is.

Help
All these gray halls
The concrete walls
Steel bars
It's so hard to C the stars
I can't roam
Please let me go home
Isolation, discrimination, aggravation
Can't they see the pain, drives me insane.
How many cries 4 help
The blind woman sees and
the deaf woman hears
the nightmares of another
woman's fears
Help, I'll ask one more time
Help.

I still vividly recall a dream I had during this time. I dreamt that I was in the back seat of a car, and the driver was driving really fast—so fast the trees were a blur. The person in the back seat with me was falling out of the door. I tried to save them, but I couldn't, and they fell out. Then I was falling out; I was desperately holding on. I was halfway out of the car holding on to the door and the other passengers in the car were trying to help me to no avail. I was slowly losing my grip. I remember my head almost hitting the trees and other things on the side of the road as we were still going fast. The moment I thought about giving up and letting go, I was able to get a grip and position myself to allow others to help me. Ultimately, "we" pulled "me" back in the car.

I believe this dream represented my journey through addiction. No one can help me unless I am willing to help myself. I also believe the dream was telling me that I was going to the bitter ends before I would be willing to help myself and allow others to help me.

One time at HALT we watched this movie called *Losing Isaiah* with Halle Berry. She was a crackhead and lost her son. There are scenes where she is smoking crack, and everybody watching the movie with me was **triggered**! We could taste that crack in our mouths; I wanted some! The counselor said, "You wish that was you right now, don't you?" Of course, she debriefed us after the movie so we could talk out those feelings.

I think watching that movie was so bad for me because I was probably already getting high at that time. There was a bar next door to the facility. I would sneak through a fence, go over to the bar, and play pool for powder cocaine. I don't know if the guys I played were letting me win. Although I am good at pool, I am not **that good**, and I am most certainly not a pool shark. I would sneak back over to HALT, and that's when I learned how to *rock the powder up* into crack. I messed up a lot of cocaine, but I learned how to do it.

One time I was in the bathroom at the facility smoking crack. I got caught. I was in the bathroom just a little too long, and they got suspicious. They had a meeting about me. For some reason, they didn't put me out; they let me stay. They probably should have put me out. That would have been best for me. Even before that, one of the counselors was telling me, "Dellenna, you're complacent."

"So, what the fuck does that mean?"

"You're just going through the motions. Basically, you've got a reservation. You're not done yet."

And I wasn't, she was right. I wrote this letter to my mother on Jan. 13, 1999.

Mom,

Hi guys. How R U doing? I'm OK. I had a little problem and relapsed over the weekend. But I'm doing good today. One of my consequences is 14-day phone restriction. So, if you're wondering why I haven't called, that's why. If it's not a problem, I need some more stamps and cigarettes. Jallanna probably won't be able to come down here until the middle of February. But anyway, I'm just taking it day by day, 24 hrs at a time. I miss you all especially Jallanna. Give her a kiss for me. Don't worry about me. I have a lot of support, my peers, staff and family. So, don't worry, I'll be OK. Everyone makes mistakes. I just made a bad decision. But I'm owning up to it and facing the consequences. I can't do anything but learn from this experience. I gotta go, we have group to go to. I'll write again soon. I love you all.

Love,
Dellenna

I totally minimized my relapse. Even though I used drugs while I was at HALT, the people running it completed me through the program. I got out of there on March 8, 1999. I went to live with my cousin Jacintha and her 9-year-old daughter in another part of Houston. When I left HALT, I had a spiritual foundation, or so I thought, just like a lot of others with a few days or weeks clean. I still had a sponsor and a wonderful support network. Everything was OK at first while I was staying with Jacintha. I went to a few twelve-step meetings. I would see my sponsor there but eventually I stopped calling her. I never did thoroughly work the twelve steps. I just touched on the first three steps.

My main focus was on getting a job, not on my sobriety. I was getting very frustrated because none of my job leads were calling me back, and I was broke. After a job interview one day, I decided to go play some pool at a bar. I was playing with a guy and sort of dumping my shit on him. I didn't know that he was the owner of the bar. He offered me a job as a waitress. During the daytime, the bar seemed like a pretty respectable place. But when I got there that evening to work, it was a totally different place. I did not know there was a titty bar next door, and the same man owned it.

Jacintha knew I was in recovery, but she didn't really understand what that meant so we would go out a lot to the clubs. She told me I looked "too dull" so she would dress me up in her clothes, but that look really wasn't me. She tried to help me, but I was really uncomfortable with Dellenna—in anybody's clothes, any environment, or any situation for that matter. Eventually, I started drinking again. My disease was telling me *alcohol is not your drug of choice, so you can drink. As long as you don't use cocaine, you'll be all right.*

Now by this time, I had stopped going to twelve-step meetings. My excuses were that I had no transportation and I worked nights, so I needed to get my sleep during the day. I had many more excuses, too. I had also lost all contact with my sponsor. And my spirituality went out the window. I went from reading my Bible every day to not reading it at all. I had no contact with my Higher Power. By this time, I was drinking and smoking marijuana every day. I was making good money waitressing. I had cash every night. Eventually I was back to snorting and smoking (cocaine) again. My cousin knew something was up. But she didn't know what.

Besides waitressing, I was making money on the pool table. I'd get some guys and they'll do anything to be in a woman's face. I'd say, "I'll bet you a game of pool" or "I'll bet you this shot." The bar owner was always trying to get me to dance next door, but I was making more money in the pool hall than the dancers. Jacintha worked days and I worked nights, so I had the house to myself. When I ran out of money to buy drugs, I would sell her daughter's TV or game device in the morning, turn a trick to get money, get some drugs, then buy it back and before Jacintha got home. One time I didn't do it in time. When she came home, her daughter's stuff was gone. I did eventually get it back but shit just started blowing up. Jacintha eventually told me I had to leave. By this time, I was getting high almost daily.

I went to live with my Uncle Don in Missouri City, southwest of Houston. I love my Uncle Don. He is one of my favorite uncles. I feel like I can do no wrong in his eyes. He has never judged me; he just always loved me.

I wrote about that time period later in a journal, when I was in yet another recovery program called New Hope Women's Center in the city of Pasadena, east of Houston.

When I was asked to leave my cousin's, I felt guilty, jealous, mad, sorry for myself and lonely. When I got to my uncle's house, I felt relieved at first, but then I was bored and lonely. I was feeling resentful towards myself because I was doing something I should not have been doing and I couldn't stop. I thought about calling someone or going to a meeting. But I didn't because I felt ashamed. I felt ashamed because my sponsor would leave messages like "I haven't seen U at meetings. I know I'll hear from U when U get in enough pain." I didn't want to show my face in a meeting for some reason. My counselor and my cousin had a bet whether or not I was going to relapse. My counselor told me I was in relapse mode the day I was leaving. I had an excuse for everything. She said I was justifying my behavior. My cousin told me she had concerns about me going to Jacintha's house. I was again justifying. I told her I would have transportation. My cousin said that car will get u in trouble. I blew it off. I told her she does not understand and she does not know what she is talking about. Eventually the car did get me in trouble.

My cuz Allan would smoke and drink with me about once a week. I was thinking about having my own $ for an apartment and car. But I was less motivated and I would get interviews (and be) too lazy to go. My self-esteem dropped. My expectations were lowered. I had intentions of going to interview but the day of the interview would come and bullshit would come up and I would either not go or reschedule. When I have positive things to do involving my sobriety, I let a lot of negative things get in the way!

When I was living with Uncle Don, I had some people over to his house one time when he was gone. I was turning tricks with them and getting drugs. While I was having sex with one guy, the others were going through the house. They stole my uncle's gun, his phone, some other things, and he came home while all of this was going on. I know he was angry with me, but he's just so calm and cool. He didn't yell at me, he just talked to me. But by that time, he was talking to a brick wall. I remember feeling so bad and thinking *how can I be so stupid?*

I stayed with my cousin Alan and his mom, Aunt Sharon, for a while. Alan and I smoked a lot of weed. He was like a brother to me. I'm a year or two older than he is. It was a tough time for both of us; he had a brother who died, and I had a brother who died. He's like my best friend and he knows me like no one else. We bonded in many ways over many things. He's into music and writes a lot of poetry or lyrics. It was poetry to me, and I loved to listen to him read it. We were very supportive of each other. I think we both needed that at that time.

One time we were arguing over something; he thought I was using again. I just left. I didn't know where I was going. I was walking down a busy street. All of the sudden I noticed that he had pulled up in his car and was calling me. "You can't come back to the house if you're going to use, and you can't stay with me and my mom."

"Fuck you."

We were arguing just being so dramatic. You would have thought he was my man. He had all my clothes in his car and was about to throw my stuff in the middle of the street. When he opened the door to get my stuff out, the door hit me in my face above my nose right between by eyes. Blood was everywhere. I saw the blood and lost it. I was screaming like I was about to die. When the police drove by and saw, Alan had a change of heart. He quickly picked up my clothes and threw them in the car. He pushed me into the car. I was screaming, "You're going to jail. I'm going to tell your mom, and my dad's gonna kick your ass." I was so mad, and he kept saying, "I'm sorry, I'm sorry."

Alan would never put his hands on me intentionally; he is not like that. He was not trying to hurt me. We would play fight and wrestle a lot, but he would never hit me.

My dad came to visit a few days later and when he saw me, he told me I should have got stitches for the cut. When I told him what I had to said to Allan. My dad said, "He should have hit your mouth."

But at that moment in our time together, Alan and I needed each other. We had so much in common. We were both in these dark places. We would read the Bible together. He was very comforting, and I know I was comforting to him. And Aunt Sharon was such a sweetheart to me.

That was one of the better times for me but those never lasted. Jacintha had introduced me to this guy named Tony and I kept in touch with him after I moved from her home. One time he and I were supposed to drive to San Antonio for the weekend. He didn't do drugs, but I wanted to get high, so in the car on the way there, I acted like a bitch. I actually acted like a bitch the entire evening--complaining, whining, and just being annoying. We ended up driving back that night. Sometime later Tony loaned me his car for the day. I dropped him off at work and was supposed to pick him up, but I never did. I was gone for a few days with his car getting high. Some guys gave me some crack and said, "Let us use the car. You stay here and you can smoke all of this." And they took the car. When they brought it back, the very expensive sound system was gone. The stereo, the speakers, everything—gone. I was like *oh shit! How could I be so dumb?* That's what they wanted to do all along—steal the sound system. I was just like *fuck, I can't bring the car back now, so what am I going to do?*

I went to a female friend's apartment, but she did not answer the door. I didn't know what else to do. I decided to fake a suicide. I needed to go somewhere. I thought the hospital would be the best place. I thought that once they admit me, I could call Tony and tell him I got car jacked or robbed or even that the car was stolen. I was scheming on some bullshit lie. I was just so tired from being up for a few days!

I ended up calling 911 from a pay phone. I told them, "There's a woman up on the balcony on the second floor outside this apartment and it looks like she's taken pills and passed out. You need to send an ambulance. She'll be here, but I won't cause I gotta go to work." I hung up and went up to the balcony. I laid down and placed pills that I'd been given for cravings strategically around me. I just laid there until the ambulance came. I kept my eyes closed and they were doing what paramedics do. I remember one guy saying, "She's not responding to the smelling salt, sir!" I wanted to laugh out loud, but I held it in.

They took me to the hospital. This nurse told me that I had to drink the "charcoal" and I told her, "I didn't take the pills!" She insisted once again for me to drink the charcoal, and I told her again, "I didn't take the pills! I'm good." She told me again to drink the charcoal, and I argued, "Ma'am, you don't understand. I did not take the pills. I am just fine." But she was not trying to hear that. She threatened me, "If you don't drink the charcoal, that man over there" (a big black security guard) "will force it down you." The "charcoal" coats your stomach to absorb the drugs. Eventually, I drank the damn charcoal, gagging at every gulp. I was peeing black for three days afterward.

They put me in the psychiatric ward. There were some clinically crazy people there. My roommate thought she was Satan. I would talk to her and say, "I don't know how you think you are Satan, I'm Satan. I've done worse things than you." She ended up going home while I was there. There was another man hearing voices. This was my first experience with some people that really had some severe mental health issues. I was like, *wow, I don't want to come back here.* But I was in there lying to everyone. I told people that I saw my brother Silas get shot and killed when I didn't. I made up this story and I believed it for a long time. The doctor diagnosed me with PTSD (Post Traumatic Stress Disorder). When I was caught up in addiction, I told myself a lot of lies. And I believed those lies at the time.

After three days in the psych ward, I was released. In May 1999, I was admitted to the New Hope Women's Center that I mentioned earlier. Here is more from the journal I wrote:

If I could have changed one thing, I would have changed my gender. I would rather be a man out there smoking my drug of choice than a woman. If I could change one thing, I wish I never would have started using in the first place. Every time I promise me and God I won't use any more, I always used. I asked God to help me. He would throw help at me but because of my pride and self-reliance, I ran to the dope man. I did the best I knew. My cousin (who worked at HALT) would call at the most fucked up times. Either when I was going to get high or when I was getting high and I blew her off when I could have asked for help. I did not ask for help because I wasn't through fuckin' up.

...

I tried to control my use of drugs by only using weekends, which did not work. When I was at a party, everybody was doing drugs. I did not want to use either of my drug of choices so I just drunk alcohol. By the end of the night, I had done every drug at the party. Another time I took Nyquil and it made me want to drink, it triggered my disease. Then my mission began, the mission which resulted in me getting what I really wanted—cocaine. And it all started with the other drugs. I could be alone and someone would come along and irritate me. When I was not under the influence, I was always easily irritated and discontent. Even though I had no intention of using, I eventually ended up using to medicate what I was feeling. I'm working on my spiritual foundation and people are irritating me and I feel frustrated and confused. I usually would go run to the dope house because I felt mad right now. But not today. I am trying to accept them for who and how they are. I am being tolerable and trying to be understanding.

...

In sobriety, NO PAIN NO GAIN. *Pain brings about Growth. If I can't face the Pain, I ain't gonna make it. So,* WRITE IT. *Today I made progress. I got off the pity pot real quick, felt what I had to feel. God grant me the serenity to accept the things I cannot change, the courage to change the things I can and the wisdom to know the difference.*

...

I've lost my self-respect by doings that I would not have done sober such as ... Having unprotected sex w/people I know nothing about. Also by sharing smoking tools. Drinking after people. Hung with people I normally would not have hung with. I went places I normally would not go. I did not take baths, teeth not brushed, hair not combed. I smelled. I stunk bad. People watched while I fucked for another hit. I also was with two men and that is not me. I feel like I got taken advantage of and I feel a loss of self, felt dirty, slutty. Right now I feel like shit.

...

I am uncomfortable sharing my feelings. When I share my feelings, I feel exposed and vulnerable. When I was in a meeting and I was not paying attention every time someone mentioned the drug of my choice by name it triggered me and really caught my attention. I got butterflies in my stomach and I started thinking about the "Good old days???" If it was that good, would I be where I am today? Hell no! I took my daughter with me to get high because I didn't want to leave her at home even though my parents were there, so I took her with me. Anything could have happened. I endangered her life. I was getting her high too because even though she was asleep, I was smoking around her.

I was making her a crack baby. Just looking back at the last few lines on the last page I feel guilty, resentful, ashamed, unmotherly like. I feel like SHIT. I feel like I do not deserve to be a mother to a child. I don't feel like finishing this assignment but a certain person told me I only have to change one thing and that's everything while allowing myself to feel my feelings. My disease is telling me to blame me but I know in reality it is my disease that is to blame. The only thing I can own up to is my actions. I endangered my life as well. I could have had an accident. I put myself in dangerous environments with dangerous and crazy people. Anything could have happened to us (me and Jallanna). I also endangered my life by having unprotected sex.

May 31, 1999:

I was afraid for another person today. She left the house and I know she was going to use. The only thing I can do is pray 4 her. I am also resentful towards her. It upsets me because she gave up so easily. She doesn't realize how serious this disease is. She's playing with fire. Next time she might not make it back. And when she left, she snuck out and didn't tell nobody. Nobody knew she was gone.

June 8, 1999:

I was afraid for another person today. She left the house very upset. She left all her clothes and someone said they saw her at the side of the highway and when they turned around to get her, she was gone.

In this same notebook, I wrote this under the title "Surrender."

Lord, I offer myself to you. I do not want to go back out. I need you, I need your help. I am surrendering myself to build with me and do with me as you will. Me and everything I have is yours. Please release me from self bondage so that I will do your will, not mine or no one else's. Help me to do your will always. Please Help me. Please Help me. Please Help me. I need you. God, you are my director. Direct and Guide me to do your will and your will only. Please Help me. If I ever needed you more, it is now. I need you in my life to guide me. Please Help me.

On June 1, 1999, my mother wrote me this letter.

Dear Dellenna,

Hope this letter finds you in good spirit. I think about you often and pray that you will get better and come back to us.

You are my only daughter and I love you very much. Keep calling when you can and we will call you.

We are not your enemies and we all love you and wish you the best. We realize only you can help yourself get better and stay on the road to recovery. We will never give up on you because we care so much about you.

You are always on our minds and in our prayers.

Enclosed is a poem for you. (Don't Quit) The road may be long and lonely but there is light at the end. Always believe in yourself and you will be OK. Know that we will always believe in you and are here to help.

Love,

Your mother and father

This poem by John Greenleaf Whittier is printed on a small card that I still have.

Don't Quit
When things go wrong as they sometimes will,
When the road you're trudging seems all up hill,
When the funds are low and the debts are high
And you want to smile, but you have to sigh,
When care is pressing you down a bit,
Rest, if you must, but don't you quit.
Life is queer with its twists and turns.
As everyone of us sometimes learns,
And many a failure turns about
When he might have won had he stuck it out;
Don't give up though the pace seems slow—
You may succeed with another blow.
Success is failure turned inside out –
The silver tint of the clouds of doubt,
And you never can tell how close you are,
It may be near when it seems so far;
So stick to the fight when you're hardest hit—
It's when things seem worst that you must not quit.

For a while at New Hope, I was doing good. I even had a job. While I was there, my mom and dad came and served me with papers for custody of Jallanna. I remember feeling so disappointed in myself—guilty and ashamed for not being mother material. I was grateful that it was family getting custody and not some strangers, but I still felt less than a woman for not taking care of my child.

I made a God Box out of a shoe box that I decorated. I never really considered myself the artsy type; I do not recall it being anything fancy. But it was my God Box. The staff told us to put all our worries in the God Box and God will take care of them. I wrote my daughter's name on a piece of paper, and that piece of paper with

Jallanna's name on it was the very first thing I put in the God Box. That act symbolized me putting my baby in God's hands. I just gave her back to God. I said, "She is yours; you take care of her; just watch over her. I'm giving her back to you."

One day my friend Lisa loaned me her car, and I had a flat tire on the way to buy drugs at this place called The Hole in Clinton Park on the east side of Houston.

I got stranded over there. I didn't really get stranded. I was getting high and the car had a flat tire, and I was trying to get it fixed so I could get the car back, but I was too busy getting high. I wasn't working too hard to get the car fixed. I was getting high in this one-bedroom little shack in a junkyard that this guy was staying in. This guy and I had a business relationship. He would bring dates in, I would turn dates for drugs, then I would pay him with drugs for using his place.

I finally brought the car back to Lisa with a spare tire on it. Because of my relapsing, I had to leave New Hope, and I had nowhere to go. I felt so guilty and ashamed that I went back to Clinton Park.

There was an older man named Alberta who had a hole in his throat. He had a house at the end of a dead-end street. It had no electricity and no heat. He didn't smoke, but that was where all the drug dealers and prostitutes went to hang out. He tricked with the prostitutes.

We had candles all over Alberta's house. We made do without the electricity. One time there was electricity for about two weeks before it was cut off again. This is one of the many places I stayed while using in this neighborhood. I was staying wherever I could. I was also staying with this man who was on dialysis. He was a drug dealer. He was in a wheelchair because he had diabetes and his legs had been cut off. At some point, I was taking care of him, not because it was the right thing to do, but because he would give me drugs.

Around this time a guy I used with, named Baytown, asked me,

"Dellenna, why don't you trick for money? Then you can go get your own drugs." I was getting bad drugs, nasty stuff. So I was like *oh, OK, that makes sense.* But a lot of people didn't want to pay me, not the drug dealers anyway. They just preferred giving me their nasty drugs; they weren't giving up the money 'cuz they knew their drugs were bad. What Baytown said made sense. I learned everything the hard way. I would turn a date and say OK, give me the money, and they would try to get over on me by not paying me. I learned to get the money upfront and to hide it. I had all these little hiding spots that people wouldn't think to look. I started out naïve to the game, to that way of life, but learned you can't trust anybody out there. Everyone has ulterior motives, and I had ulterior motives, too. "How can you benefit me?" The only reason I would mess with people is if there was something in it for me.

Like the guy with the shack in the junkyard. I benefited by using his shack. Mind you, I never had a pimp. Crack was my pimp. I had a problem with doing what I did and giving my money to someone. That just wasn't me. I'd do what I did and get my money for crack.

I remember this one dude, a drug dealer, who was my age and really fine. He was trying to take me back to treatment. "Do you want help?" he asked me. I was like "yeah". He told me he would take me back to treatment. "I'll come pick you up at this time." He waited outside that shack. Mind you, he was selling drugs while he was waiting, 'cuz that was where people came to get their drugs. I was in the shack smoking, and he kept saying, "Are you ready yet?"

"No, just one more."

But he waited out there all day, and finally he said, "When you're ready, let me know, and I'll take you to get you the help that you need."

He didn't use drugs himself. He had a baby and a girlfriend and a house. He was just a stand-up guy. There were a lot of drug dealers over there trying to help me. They didn't have any problem taking my money for drugs. But they were still trying to help me. I was new to the community at first, and they would say things like "You don't need to be over here, you're too pretty for this." And I'd say, "Are you going to give me some or not? I got money—what the fuck? I'm not trying to hear that shit you're saying, I'm trying to get high."

Even though they wanted to help me, they were not going to turn down my money because of their addiction, which was money. They could have gotten legitimate jobs, some did have jobs and sold drugs on the side. But selling drugs is quick money; the lifestyle can be addictive as well. There are a lot of drug dealers who are extremely smart. To be a drug dealer is to be a businessman; selling drugs is a business. If they are business-minded, drug dealers, prostitutes, or any salesperson in that lifestyle knows how to keep their customers happy, therefore keeping their buyers' business. It takes a set of skills to keep your clientele up; however, those living that lifestyle are not using their skill in a way that would benefit them legally. I have a unique set of skills as well.

I ended up staying with the guy who didn't have any legs. He kinda took a liking to me. I would bathe him and take care of him, mainly because he had drugs and I could get high whenever I wanted. But I've always had a heart. Like I was the type of person, even if I didn't like you, if you were hungry and I had something, I would feed you even though we might have physically fought last week. I did that a lot. My mom always told me, if someone's hungry, you feed them. So, I did that. People just thought I was naïve, but I had a heart. That's one thing I never lost. People used to say, "There's something about you, I don't know what it is, but you don't belong out here." Nobody was able to tell me what that something was. The mentality of the streets is do or die, survival of the fittest, that was never my motto I just wanted to survive without hurting anyone in the process.

One time when I was in Minnesota, this woman attacked me. She was pinning me down, but I had something sharp in my hand and I jabbed it in her neck. I could have killed her, like *fuck this bitch up*, but something inside me said, *Just jab her enough to get her off you, don't kill her.* That's what I did. She got off me, and that was that.

There was always something inside me that said, *Don't hurt people.*

I really do think it was the God in me, His love, because God is love. Unfortunately, in my sick way of thinking, it was OK for me to hurt myself, but not others. I have a love for human beings that addiction couldn't even take from me. I think that's what was different about me. I just automatically loved human beings. I'm not saying that didn't stop me from doing a lot of things and hurting a lot of people. But I would never take someone's life. Yeah, even if I felt they deserved it, I wouldn't, 'cuz that's just not me. Like the people who raped me—I learned to forgive them by praying for them. It didn't happen right away, so I had to keep praying. Everything I wanted for myself, I would pray that they receive. I told God, *You know I don't mean a word of this shit, but I'm just trying to do the right thing.* God knew my heart. I would talk to Him periodically. I cared about people. But I had ulterior motives. It wasn't like I was altruistic out there. I always got something in return, like when I took care of the man on dialysis. I had a college education and a lot of people out there didn't. Not to say I was better or not to say I didn't belong out there because nobody belongs out there. I was different because I was not brought up like that; my parents instilled morals and values in me. I knew better.

In the Clinton Park community in Texas, I stayed wherever I could; I didn't have a permanent home. One time when I was staying with the guy with no legs, a constable came to the house and told me my brother was looking for me. I thought, *How in the world did my brother find me in the big ass state of Texas?* The constable was a good guy. One time I hit a *big lick*, a come up. I ran into a man who had a lot of money; eventually I got the money. Afterward, I was sitting on the corner in tears, and I didn't want to use that night. The constable walked up to me and asked, "What's wrong?"

"I don't have anywhere to sleep tonight, and I have all this money and I don't want to get high."

That constable went out of his way to take me to somebody's house, a place that he thought would be safe for me to stay. What he didn't know was I got high with that individual too. I was always honest with him; I was always honest with the police, about the obvious shit. This constable was just a really good man. He would always ask me, "What are you doing out here?"

As I said before, I never lied to the police about the obvious shit; they would roll up on me while I was standing on the corner sometimes, and they would ask me, "What are you doing?"

My response would be "You know I'm not out here waiting on the bus. You might want to move down a little bit 'cuz you're fucking up my groove." I would always tell them, "I know you guys have a job to do, and I know what I'm doing is against the law, but I know you guys have something more to do, like fighting crime, than to be watching me here on this corner." If a trick and I would get pulled over by the police, I would say to the John, "You need to tell the truth about you picking me up because they know me, they know what I do. Or better yet, let me do the talking." I would never admit to having drugs, I would always tell the police: "Officer, I was on my way to cop, but I ran into you and you fucked that up." Then I would turn around and ask them, "By the way, do you know where the good dope is? I know you guys know where the good dope is." I found that if I had drugs on me and I started a conversation with the police, I would be less suspicious, and they would think that I didn't have any drugs on me. I'd never act suspicious. I always engaged in conversation. Like I said, there are some good police and there are some asshole police too. I was out there long enough to figure out who was who.

I remember one time a trick and I got pulled over right after copping—a lot of tricks smoked crack—and I explained, "Tell him the truth about trickin' with me, but do not tell him we have any drugs." I had the drugs on me and well, he decided to lie and tell the officer he picked me up because I needed a ride, the officer knew me and knew that was a lie. The officer asked me what was going on. I told him, "He picked me up for some head and we were going to cop some crack, but we can't find any, we might as well just mosey along." Well, needless to say, the man I was with was taken into custody for lying and I was let go—with the drugs. I just had a way with the police officers. But they didn't always let me off as you'll see later.

That nice constable would sometimes bring me breakfast from a Jack in the Box that was close by. But I wasn't too worried about food when I was using. Sometimes people would feed me. Baytown's family lived on the outskirts of the neighborhood, and sometimes we would go over there and get something to eat. His mom would always let us in and feed us. Baytown also had a girlfriend whose house we would go to. I could tell at one time she was beautiful, but the drugs had done a number on her. I remember sitting at her house and staring at her and thinking, *I don't want to be an old ho. I don't want to be 50, 60 years old standing on the corner. I don't want to do that.*

She had custody of her mom who was confined to a bed. Her mom would be in the back of the house yelling and in so much pain 'cuz she needed to be changed, or she was thirsty or hungry. But we would be too busy up in the front getting high. I just can't imagine being confined to a bed in a room like that all the time knowing everyone's out in front getting high, taking your belongings, and you've messed your pants and need to be changed, but you can't do anything for yourself. So, sometimes I would go back there and change her and talk to her, give her something to drink. When you're living on an animalistic level like we were, you don't think about other people. It is about survival and getting what you want. It was sad to see that woman like that, and sometimes I wonder what happened to her.

I'd also stay at Alberta's house because I would help him. He had a hole in his throat and used an electronic larynx held up to his throat to speak. There were a lot of drug dealers in that community. I would trick with them, and they would try to get me to stay with them, but I just couldn't be kept. I didn't want to be controlled and I didn't want anyone to help me. They weren't helping me anyway if they were getting me high. But of course, they knew they couldn't stop me although one trick tried.

This trick had just bought a house up on the end of the hill. I had been staying with him off and on. One day he woke me up and he said to me, "You're not leaving today." I didn't pay him no mind and went back to sleep. I just wanted to chill that day anyway. When I finally woke up, I noticed he was gone and I was locked in the house. His house had bars in the windows and he had put a padlock on the outside of the door. And he had two big ass pit bulls outside. I thought to myself, *No, this BITCH didn't, I'm gonna show this mother fucker.* I found a window where the bars were loose, so I worked at it for a while, and I was small enough to crawl out. The dogs were barking furiously but thank God they didn't bite me. I didn't run, I just calmly backed away. When I'm locked and loaded like that, nothing is going to stop me. Besides, I actually love dogs. The two dogs were not vicious; they just had a mean bark. The guy later came and found me and asked , "How did you get past the dogs?" I knew not to go back to his home. He wasn't gonna be lockin' me in again.

One particular guy I used with was such an asshole. When you have drugs, you're like the king or queen—you have all the power. The asshole would talk shit and put everyone down when he had drugs. When he didn't have drugs, he was a begging lowlife. One time he hit a *big lick* and had some money and drugs, so he had asked me to go with him. I didn't really want to go because of the way he treated people when he had the upper hand; however, I was desperate, so I went. We went to the store and ended up getting a hotel room—me, him, and another girl. He was being an asshole, and I somehow ended up with his credit card in my possession. I don't remember how I stole his credit card, but I did and no one knew. I even pretended to help him look for it. "When's the last time you used it?" I asked him. "Maybe you left it there." By the time we got back to the neighborhood, everyone knew his card was missing. I did not want to be a suspect, so I stuck around for a while. The girl that was with us left as soon as we got back. I was dying laughing inside, especially when I hooked up with Zeke, this older man I knew wouldn't tell. We used the credit card to pay for hotel rooms; we were living large. This guy wasn't sure it was me who stole his card, but he just kinda assumed 'cuz I was gone for a while, and I was coming back with stuff, like clothes. He thought it was me, but I told him, "I know how to make money too. I just caught a *big lick*. I don't need your card."

I remember one night he told me to get in his car with him. We were driving way out from the city, and he was saying, "One of the things I don't like is a thief and a liar." He wasn't sure I had the card, so he was fishing. He did not have any drugs that night, but I had some drugs on me and I was just listening to him. I said, "If I had your card, I would just be gone. I would not be coming back. Besides, I am the one that stayed with you when we got back in town, your li'l girlfriend was the one that left with the quickness, but I don't think it was her either. Maybe you just lost it." To distract him even further, I told him, "I have some shit, do you want a hit?" I said all this stuff to lead him to believe me. Somehow, I convinced him because I really think he was taking me out there to hurt me. I talked my way out of situations a lot of times.

We ended up coming back into the city. He never said anything to me about the card after that. I did feel bad when I heard him on the phone with his sister, and I found out it was his sister's credit card I'd been using. I thought to myself, "This isn't even your card, like if this had been your card, this shit would have been OK." He stole it from her. So, I stopped using the card. I didn't want to hurt her; I wanted to hurt him because he was an asshole.

I would find spots in abandoned houses and just sit there and get high and think alone. I didn't want to be with anyone. Because of the things I had to do to get my drugs, I was absolutely not sharing. "You don't know what I had to do to degrade myself, dehumanize myself" was my way of thinking. One time I woke up and I had started breaking out, and I started scratching. I got a guy to go to a pay phone and call 911. I went to the hospital and they diagnosed me with shingles. They kept me in an enclosed room because I was contagious. I was there for three weeks. They had never seen anyone in their 30s get shingles. It was so painful. They gave me morphine; I didn't like the feeling the morphine gave me. I don't like opiates. I'd only use them to come down off the crack but not just because.

I remember these two young female doctors came in to see me. I was always honest with doctors and nurses. "I do drugs," I told them. They asked me if I wanted help and I told them, "I really don't think there is any help for me right now. The most you can do for me is pray 'cuz I'm not done yet." Even before I went to Texas, I remember telling my mom, "Just pray, just pray. Pray that I survive 'cuz I'm tired of getting your hopes up, my hopes up, everyone's hopes up, only to let them down. I'm just gonna get this shit out of my system and just pray that I survive."

I did touch base with my parents when I was in the hospital. I usually didn't have a lot of contact with them. I would check in with them maybe two times every six months, if even that. I knew they were looking for me though. Like I said, my brother had talked to the constable who patrolled the community I was using in. Most of the time they didn't know whether I was dead or alive. When I called my parents from the hospital, my mom didn't even believe me 'cuz of all my lies in the past. I don't blame her. My parents called the hospital and verified that I was there. When I left the hospital, I went to my cousin's house and my dad drove all the way from Minnesota to Texas to see me. He spent the day with me. We played dominoes, watched TV, and shot a few games of pool. He left me some money for my medication and went to my uncle's house. I took the money and disappeared. My dad stayed for a whole month hoping and praying that I was OK. He didn't see me again before he finally went back to Minnesota. I felt ashamed to even call and let my parents know I was alive.

I went back to Clinton Park and Baytown connected me to this young woman who had recently been released from jail. She was cute. When you come out of jail, you're cute again 'cuz you got all your weight back. She put me down on the truck stops; she let me know that is where I could make some easy money. Some of the truck drivers wanted women and others wanted women and drugs.

I had a habit of telling people, "I'll be right back," and then I'd be gone a week with these truck drivers. One time I told Alberta, "I'll be right back, going to the store." I was picked up by a trucker and I came back a month later. Alberta snorted when he saw me. "Where'd you go? You said you'd be right back."

There was one truck driver that I'd go on the road with, and everywhere we went we'd get high. That's where I learned about EFS (Electronic Fund Source) checks and compensation checks. When we ran out of cash, he would get these EFS or comp checks where the company paid him in advance, and when he dropped the load off, he would pay them back. I learned a lot about the truck stops. The prostitutes were called *lot lizards*. I would be on the CB radio: "Anybody lonely? Holla at Lovely, channel 16." Lovely was one of my handles. I never gave people my real name. I would come back to the truck with money after turning a trick, and this driver would get on the CB to find drugs. They have code words for certain drugs. "Chicken feet" was crack. We'd find some drugs that way and get high. This driver was a white guy in his 40s or 50s. He told me he used to be a senator; I don't know if that was true. Everyone's got a story. I was like *whatever, senator-turned-trick-truck-driver*, but anything's possible.

One time he came through Clinton Park looking for me, and I was like "what you got?" He'd sold his CB; he didn't have any money. I'm like "Why the fuck did you coming looking for me, and you don't have any money or a CB that I could make money off of?" But then I asked him, "What are you hauling?"

"I got beer."

Now we're talking. We went to the back of the junkyard, parked his trailer, and sold all the beer. And then we got high. He called his company and told them someone stole his load. He was desperate. Before this incident, I had traveled all over the country with him. Sometimes I would just go to get away. We weren't getting high all the time but when we stopped at truck stops, we were getting high. I would bring books to read. One time when we were in California, he found this drug spot where we were getting high for a while before he went to drop his load off, and he said for me to stay there at the house. I'm like "You're not leaving me in California." I stayed for a while and when the drugs were gone, I left. I'm very resourceful, so I found out where he was dropping off his load, and I found him. We went to Miami, to Louisiana—everywhere we went, we got high. We were partners in crime, but when he sold his CB, *that's it!* I thought, *this relationship is severed.* "Don't you ever come lookin' for me if you don't have any money, I can't do anything for you," I told him.

I hooked up with another truck driver. He was a black guy. I always knew his truck 'cuz he had a black diamond on the side. We used to have really good conversations. Everybody has their different *tweak* when they get high. Like some people can't talk after they get high; some people will pick up knives. I would just talk. I guess that's what kept some of my tricks coming back 'cuz I was able to get high and hold a normal conversation with them. This truck driver would say, like everybody else did, "You don't belong out here." *Like anyone belongs out here*, I would think.

I had him park in the empty field across from Alberta's house, and I would go to Alberta's house to buy our drugs. On Jan. 14, 2000 I bought some drugs and came back to the truck, and there comes that damn constable. He had us get out of the truck. He's searching the truck, and we didn't have any drugs at that time because they had already been smoked. But I had a little makeup case that I kept my crack in with the razor. The constable found it. I knew I had licked that shit up and thought there was no freakin' crack on there. But he ran a test, and it turned a certain color, so he knew it was residue. I ended up going to jail.

The truck driver was doing crack, too, but I told the constable, "It's me." It's not like I took it for him, but he had a family. I said to the constable, "It's a makeup case, do you think he would have a makeup case?" It was my first charge in Texas. I'd been caught for prostitution there but nothing like this. The constable told me, "You'll just go to jail for 30 to 60 days because it's your first charge." Little did he know the judge sentenced me to six months for some freaking crack dust. Disappearing from my friends like that was an extended "I'll be right back."

4

Don't mess with Texas

When they say, "Don't mess with Texas!" they really mean it. I got sentenced to spend six months in the Plane State Jail, a minimum-security prison northeast of Houston. I spent some time in the county jail before *pulling chain* (being moved to the state jail).

There were a lot of people coming into the county jail. People came in for simply having *stems* (crackpipes) and other paraphernalia in their possession. It was sad. There were also mothers in there because their children weren't going to school. Parents got arrested and, depending on how many times they'd been arrested for their children being truant, they could go to prison, which ultimately led to them losing their jobs. That was crazy.

In the county jail, we made *hooch* (moonshine). We took fruit and bread and fermented it. I bought other inmates' medications—trazadone (anti-depressant), Percocet (opioid) and some other stuff and put that in the *hooch*.

Before being moved to Plane State in March, two months after I was arrested, I was asking the other inmates about what to expect. They told me I'd be assigned a job like the *hoe squad*, which is the female version of the chain gang. Women with hoes moved rocks from one side of the yard in the hot Texas sun, then they moved them back over to the other side of the yard. They also worked in the laundry and had administrative jobs.

I didn't want to be on the *hoe squad*, so I asked the other inmates how to get out of that. They told me I would be assigned a job, and something had to be physically wrong with me in order not to be assigned the *hoe squad*. So, when my name was called at 3:00 a.m. to be moved from the county jail to Plane State, I grabbed the arm sling that one of the other inmates had and put it on.

I tried to "play the part," but I didn't know how because my arm wasn't really hurt. They shackled our feet, chained our hands, and bused us to Plane State. When we got there, we had to strip down butt naked. Then we had to line up and bend over and spread our butt cheeks. The guards walked down the line looking up our butts. I think they did that only to humiliate us. It was dehumanizing. Then they threw us each a bar of soap to wash away any lice or bed bugs, and they hosed us down like a herd of animals. This entire time, I was still trying to "play the part," limiting the movement of my arm.

From there, we went to the reception area where inmates were housed until they figured out their housing dorm and job assignment. I didn't know that they were going to make us go to the infirmary. When I found that out, I thought shit, *I'm busted,* they're going to find out nothing is wrong with my arm. They gave me this bootleg physical; prison physicians ain't shit and the physicals aren't that thorough. Maybe they didn't care. This man took an X-ray of my arm and said, "So, you got a hairline fracture."

I was secretly shocked but went along with it. I was like "Yeah. I fell off the top bunk." I don't know what the hell he saw. There was nothing wrong with my arm!

But I messed myself up faking the injury because they didn't give me a job since I had a broken arm. I was pretty much confined to the dorm. I went to the infirmary and the library a lot to hang out. That was really all I could do. I secretly met up with other inmates at both places. The library was my favorite place. I did a lot of reading, especially mythology, which I love. When I got to the prison, I had met a woman named Poochie. She started calling me Paper Doll, so we were known as Poochie and Paper Doll. Poochie looked like a dude. If Poochie was really a dude, Poochie would have been *fine.* I'm not gay but out of necessity, I've been with women to support my habit. But Poochie and I never had sex. We pretty much talked and wrote letters to each other.

In my dorm there were four pods, and in every pod, there were about 50 to 60 bunk beds lined up on the wall, which makes for 50 to 60 women in one pod. Every bunk bed was in a little cubicle, and we each had one drawer for our personal stuff. In the middle of all four pods was a circular picket where the guards were. They could see into all four pods—the bunk beds and all the way back into the showers and the bathrooms—and we could see them. Sometimes the dorms got shook down. The guards would come in and tear up everything. They'd flip mattresses over, go through our drawers, and throw everything in the middle of the floor so we couldn't tell whose stuff was whose.

The guards in the picket could see us changing our clothes, and some of the women changed in front of them or got out of the shower naked for them. That guard had a job to do and he had authority. If he was getting aroused, he needed to check that. Apparently, the guards didn't see it that way. They thought it was an invitation.

There was a lot of sexual harassment from the guards. The way the guards talked to us was very demeaning. There were women coming up pregnant, and they had been in jail for years. There were no Virgin Marys in there. The sexual harassment wasn't only from the men; there were female guards who were gay.

Although these inmates liked to think they were willingly having sex with the guards, they didn't understand that with the structure of power and authority, sex was technically rape. Every guard had power over us. Try to say "no" to a guard and see what happens. But none of the guards got in trouble.

I didn't have any problems like that with the guards; I cussed a few of them out and got in trouble for it, that's all. But it was humiliating the way the guards treated us.

One time I had a problem with another inmate. I don't remember what we were arguing over, but she had done some shit to me. She didn't get in trouble for it. The night before I was to be released, I put some peanut butter and some hair grease on her sheets. The guard came to me and said, "Let me see your container of grease," and she saw where my fingers had gouged out a big clump of grease. I was like *fuck, I'm busted.* I had to spend the night in a single cell. I got wrote up for that. I saw a lot of fights, but I didn't get into fights. I pretty much kept to myself. When inmates fought, the guards didn't break it up. They followed the inmates around with a video camera and the rest of us had to get in our bunks.

There was a high rate of AIDS and hepatitis C at Plane State. If there was blood on the floor after a fight, there was a special solution we had to use to clean it up.

Prison was traumatizing. The very thing that led to my incarceration—my drug use—was never even addressed. I wasn't there long enough to go to school; I wasn't there long enough to do anything. They had a twelve-step program but it was run by inmates. I went there only to get out and secretly meet up with people. Mind you, there were some people in there who were serious about their recovery but I was not at the time.

Drugs were easily accessible. It was easy to hide them because women have two "purses." I bought medications from inmates paying them with a bag of noodles or something. I also abused instant coffee in there. You can get a real good buzz off that, but it acted like a laxative, too.

While locked up the most valuable things were getting mail and receiving money from relatives for the commissary. We could always tell who didn't have any access to the outside world and who didn't have any commissary. There were some women in there who never got mail or commissary. I was grateful that my parents and family pretty much took care of me when I was in there. They sent me money. I lived off peanut butter and jelly sandwiches because I didn't like the food. I did like the peanut butter pancakes; I had never had peanut butter pancakes until I went to prison.

Having your name called during the mail roll call was an honor. I wrote a lot of letters to people I didn't know, corresponding with men in other prisons. I got their contact information from other inmates. Getting mail is almost better than getting commissary in prison; everyone anxiously waits for their name to be called when the mail comes. By writing other men in prisons, I made sure my name was called daily for receiving mail.

Although I was getting mail from guys in prisons, the best letters I received were from my family. I was excited to hear from my family. I was also happy to be able to write letters and draw pictures and send them to my daughter. I know my mother read them to her.

February 2000

Jallanna,

Hey Baby Girl, How R You? I'm hanging in there. I miss you so much. I wanted 2 tell you I love you. I think about you all of the time. I talk about you also. I look at the moon every night before I go to bed. I bet you're getting big. Please send me some pictures. I know I told you I will be there before your birthday. I am going to do everything I can 2 be there. I truly believe in my heart I will be there. I pray for God to give you a kiss from an Angel from me every night. I always pray you have sweet dreams. I miss your beautiful smile. I also miss getting the giggles with your silly butt. But write me a letter. Remember to look at the moon and I'll be looking at the same moon. Mommy loves you and misses you.

Love,

Mama

April 12, 2000

Dear Dellenna,

Jallanna did get the drawing of footprints that you sent her, and yes, she does like everything that you send her. You are very special to her and she loves you and misses you so very much.

Please keep on doing the right thing and stay on track. Use the time well and try and read and keep up to date on what is going on. I know that you will be able to make it through this situation because we are very strong black women. I am so sorry for what has happened to you but as the saying goes, things happen for a reason. It could be that God is testing us, and you have to be strong and make the right decisions and thank God that you are alive and well. Not where you would like to be but safe for now.

Keep in mind that we, your family, love you with all our heart and we'll always love you and care for you and like I have told you before, we are not your enemies and have always wanted the best for you.

Call when you can and keep your spirits up. We love you and miss you.

Love,

Mom and Dad

P.S. I will sit down with Jallanna and have her write you a letter.

I cherish this next letter from my brother, Paul.

May 22, 2000

Dellenna,

I apologize for taking so long to write back to you. I have been busy trying to finish school while working full time. Well, after 6 years, I've finally done it, I graduated from the University of Minnesota on May 17th. Jallanna was there in your place since you couldn't make it. She is so funny. Every time a camera came out, she tried to get into the picture. As you can see, she has grown into a very beautiful little girl. (There was a small photo of Jallanna included in the letter.)

Last week I saw you and her when I helped execute a search warrant with the SWAT team. We entered the house and began yelling "Get on the ground, police!" After securing all the rooms, I returned to a bedroom where there was a light-skinned black female and her baby lying on the bed. The room was disgusting and not a place where they should be lying down. She said she didn't smoke, but her physical appearance said she did. She wasn't ready to hear what I had to say, so I treated her with respect, wished her well and left.

Everywhere I go, I see you. Everywhere I go, I help you. Last winter two prostitutes needed a ride so I gave them one. I know, the police are not supposed to be a taxi service, but I knew if I was smoking crack and out on the street, my sister would do it for me. I tell you this because it is important that you know that I think about you every day.

You asked for forgiveness. I forgave you a long time ago. My only prayer and hope is that you can forgive yourself. I have not always done the right thing, and just like you, I've made mistakes. However, it is never too late to get back on track. You simply have to want a good life with your family and friends more than crack, marijuana, alcohol, tobacco, and other drugs.

Do you want your daughter to experience the things you have or do you want to take your rightful place in her life as her mother and protector? Make a choice and do it. It will be hard, but you can do it.

During the war there were times I thought I would die. I said fuck it, I'm kickin' somebody's ass and going home; I did go home, too. You have to decide what is more important, crack and the horrible life that goes with it or family, especially Jallanna. She needs you more than you can imagine. Grandparents are not parents. They have and are doing an excellent job, but J needs you as her mother. Mommy is the one you really need to thank. She keeps J involved in dance, soccer, swimming, church, choir, and other things. Also, everyone speaks positively to her about you. Yes, she is nosy and hears adult conversations she should not, but she does.

Things will be very different when you return. My girlfriend is moving out in June 1 because I'm not ready to get married. We may get back together later, but I need to figure out what I want to do with my life. Things are cool between us but she doesn't want to break up. She does appreciate that you mention her in the letters and hopes that you will make good choices and get better.

When you return, I will help you as much as possible, but you are the one who has to make the right choices and decisions. You're right, actions do speak louder than words. Show yourself, us and others that you can be the great person we know you to be.

You're funny; your letter said "Laugh, Paul," and it was about the same time I missed your jokes. Well, I'm looking forward to you returning. Take care, do sit-ups, push-ups and jog in place to not get fat.

Take care,

Love, Paul

P.S. My sister isn't a demon, she is a human who made mistakes and is ready to humble herself, ask for help, and take responsibility for her actions.

As you can see, my family really supported me and cared about my well-being.

There were a lot of people who got out of the jail and then came right back. And of course, I was talking shit about them.

When I got out after six months, my mother, my father, and Jallanna came from Minnesota to get me. I hadn't seen them since they brought me to Texas to live. I didn't want them to visit me while I was in prison; even the visitors had to be almost strip searched. I didn't want my family going through that.

When I saw my daughter after not seeing her for a year and a half, I told her I'd never leave her again. But the day we were supposed to leave to go back to Minnesota, I disappeared.

We had gone to a get-together at a family member's house, and I reconnected with a dealer from Clinton Park. I called to tell him I was out of jail. He came to pick me up and we left. No one knew where I was. We had planned on hanging out, but I left and went on a binge. My family ended up leaving without me. I didn't tell them that I did not want to go back to Minnesota. I found out later that, after I disappeared, my dad cried. Everybody thought he was crying about me, but he was crying because he didn't know how he was going to tell Jallanna that I wasn't coming home with her due to my addiction.

I was gone for about a month before I contacted anyone. I couldn't bring myself to call anyone to let them know I was OK because I was too ashamed. I let myself and everyone else down again.

My Dad's family tried so hard to help me. At one point, I stayed with my dad's cousin Fonzo and his son in Acres Homes, a neighborhood in northwest Houston. I ended up relapsing, and Fonzo knew it; he was in recovery. He said to me, "Dellenna, I got some good news and some bad news for you. Which do you want to hear first?"

"Give me the bad news."

"This thing isn't about you. You doing all this and wasting people's time. You got some people praying for you. They got a connection with God, and God is not going to let them down. This isn't even about you."

"What the hell is the good news?

"You got some people praying for you that's got a connection with God, and God is not going to let them down."

I was like "whatever."

From there I ended up using, and if Fonzo had been in his right mind, he would have put me out. I left. I was homeless by choice because all of my dad's family was down there in Texas. I could have lived with one of them.

I was wandering. I got tired of hurting my family. I was down there doing what I do—getting high, going from shelter to shelter. I met a lot of good people in the shelters.

I eventually ended up back in Clinton Park. My friends were glad to see me. A female! I got with Baytown and Alberta and all of them. Because Alberta didn't want any of my drugs—he didn't get high—I gave him money for helping me and letting me stay at his house.

I met this guy who had recently gotten out of prison after doing about fifteen years. He had moved back in with his mother who lived in the neighborhood. He was selling drugs while still on parole. I did turn tricks but not as much as before because this guy gave me drugs. I was staying with the dude with one leg who was on dialysis and he was giving me drugs. Very seldom did I have to go out.

I really wanted to stop using. I was writing in a journal. I was praying to God. I was tired of this shit. One time I prayed and cried myself to sleep. When I woke up, there was a big ass crack rock lying next to me. I don't know where it came from, who put it there, but that was not what I prayed for. It was like the devil was always busy. To this day, I don't know who put the crack there. That shit wasn't there when I went to sleep. Even though I went to bed not wanting to get high, when I woke up and saw that, I was like *fuck it.* Once I smoked that, I was off to the races.

I even tricked with a pastor. They called him the Pussy Man. We had sex on the altar in the church, and I felt really bad doing that. Afterwards, I talked to him about the Bible and joining his church, and he told me, "If you join my flock, you know we can't do this."

I thought, *You fucking hypocrite.* I asked him, "Then how I am going to pay my tithes?" He refused to give me a Bible, so I stole one later. Then he pulled out this dildo and said, "I'll give you some more money if you stick this up my ass."

Uh huh. I had money and drugs, so I declined. I was already feeling shameful and guilty about the whole experience taking place in the church. But if I had been desperate, I would have done it. This was God's house, and I was like *I can't do this* because I was always brought up to respect God's house. There was a sign outside the damn church that said, "God listens…Do you?" That sign always touched me because I knew I was not doing God's will. Through my experiences, I have learned not to put religious leaders on pedestals. I've tricked with a whole lot of pastors and religious leaders. They're human; they're not perfect. They're human just like me.

I was still in Clinton Park, using. A lot of dealers smoked *wet*—dipping cigarettes or joints in embalming fluid. Dealers talked down about people smoking crack, but I saw people who smoked *wet* get butt naked and crawl home. I am not saying one drug is better than the other, but I have never seen anyone on crack do that. That *wet* freezes your brain. You're aware of what's going on but you can't do anything, like you can't move.

One day I saw this car moving very slowly down the road. I go up to the car, I see who's driving it, and he's got all this crack on the passenger seat. He was high off that *wet* and was like in a frozen state, almost like a zombie. I got in on the driver's side and pushed him over and parked the car to get him off the street. Then I told him, "I'm taking a few of these (crack rocks) and the rest I'm going to put in the glove box, so the cops don't see it in plain view it they come up to the car." I saw him a day or two later, and he thanked me. I told him, "You know, I took some of your shit," and he said, "Yeah, I know."

"You better be glad I didn't take it all." I purposely locked his car's doors so I couldn't come back and get the rest because I'd do some shit like that. I left him in there, slumped over.

The dealers thought they were better than me because they were dipping weed in embalming fluid, but that shit is worse than crack. They called it "get wetted up" or "water world."

They also made "lean", which is where you mix soda pop with cough syrup that has codeine and promethazine in it. We poured flavored pop like grape, orange, or strawberry over crushed ice, put in the "lean," and added Jolly Rancher sticks. That helped me come down off the cocaine. It slowed me down.

One day—Jan. 29, 2001 to be exact—I was hangin' at the house of the same guy who had recently got out of prison. That was a stupid thing for me to do because I knew the police were watching him. I was getting high when the police raided the house. His poor mom—the cops had her face down on the floor. When I heard them come in, I stuck my *stem* in a hole in the wall. But I forgot that I had a piece of rubber in my purse. I used to take the rubber part off pens, that part used to help you grip the pen, and put them on the end of my *stems* so I wouldn't burn my lips. A lot of times, the stem cracked and got really short. I had to take care of my lips because my lips were my moneymakers. I used to say, "If something happens to my lips, I'll be in the unemployment line."

I had used this one piece of rubber a couple times, and it didn't work right, so I got another one, and I don't know why, but I put that other piece in my purse. When the police searched my purse, they found the piece of rubber and ran a test on it. They found residue and on Feb. 23, 2001, I was sentenced to seven months in jail. About two weeks later, I was once again transferred to Plane State Jail.

I was charged with possession, less than a gram, but that was my second felony. I went to the county jail again. I called my parents to let them know. It was the first time they had heard from me in a long while. I had missed Thanksgiving, Christmas, and New Year's with them.

Then I went back to Plane State. But this time they sent me to a TC program, a Therapeutic Community program.

When I first went in there, I had problems following the rules; I had problems with authority. The day I got there, I dropped off my state jail-issued belongings and went to the infirmary. I got in trouble because I was not supposed to leave after arriving in the dorm. The TC program has an entire set of different rules than the regular state jail.

The first morning I woke up to "cock-a-doodle-do" "yeehaw, yeehaw" and all these animal sounds. *Oh my God, where am I and what is going on?* I found out later that those sounds being made by the inmates were "consequences." If you didn't have your feet on the floor at 6 a.m., the next day you had to wake everyone else up with an animal noise. That way, the counselor can hear who's up. "So-and-so is the cow; so-and-so is the pig. I didn't hear the chicken, so she's in trouble again." The counselors tore you down to build you back up. I didn't understand then, and I still don't, how you can tear someone down who's already torn down. You're already fuckin' broken from the streets, the lifestyle, the shame and the guilt, what are they going to tear down?

In the TC program, there was a hierarchy of service we had to do. We started out cleaning the bathrooms, but we could work up to better jobs. For every negative behavior we did, our peers or the counselors could drop a ticket on you. They had an accountant keep track of the consequences and the tickets. On Tuesdays and Thursdays, we had what they called "confrontation." The inmates and one of the counselors sat in a circle. We'd be wearing our uniforms (tight whites we called them) and our black boots. We had to sit with our feet on the floor and our hands on the top of our thighs. Another counselor sat in a chair in the middle of the circle. Opposite her was an empty chair. The counselor would take the box with all the tickets in it and pull one out. If she called your name, you had to sit in the empty chair. She'd then confront you on your negative behavior that was noted on the ticket. She called my name quite a few times. One time when she called my name, I got up and walked to the chair in the middle of the circle and took a seat. She said, "Dellenna, on this date you said this to the guard, and you cursed at the guard. Do you own it or disown it?" meaning did you do it or not do it? I was so rebellious, I would say "I own it and I disown it. I did cuss the guard out but that's not what I said. This is what I said…"

My consequence for cussing the guard out was brushing my teeth three times a day. Each time after I brushed my teeth, I had to go to the middle of the floor and yell, "My mouth is now clean, and I will not use foul language." The other inmates would yell "the family accepts" or "the family does not accept." If the family accepted, I could stop. If they didn't, I had to go brush my teeth and make the announcement again. Sometimes I was brushing my teeth more than eight times a day because nobody liked me at first. If the family accepted, I'd say things like, "That doesn't mean I can't do this," and I'd stick up my arm and flick everyone off with my middle finger.

My attitude was *I'm not doing this shit* but what I didn't realize is I was getting myself into more trouble and getting more and more consequences. I had to wear a paper bag on my head that had "I'm dumb" printed on it. I had to walk around with a sign that said, "I don't listen." How was this helping with my drug problem? It wasn't. Whenever my counselor gave me a consequence, I'd say "I'm not doing it." Or I'd do it but in such a way to make everyone laugh. My counselor might tell me to sing a certain song, and I'd sing a different one. I was very creative at getting back.

One day when I was talking to my counselor, an inmate walked by wearing waders and she smelled like shit. I asked my counselor what that inmate was doing. "She's cleaning out the poo-poo pond."

"What's the poo-poo pond?"

"That's where all the sewage from the toilets comes in, and you have to take the sanitary napkins out. The next rule you break, that's what you're gonna be doing."

I thought to myself, *Hell to the naw.* It was at that moment that I thought it would be beneficial to me to not be so rebellious.

My counselor told me: "Dellenna, everywhere you go, you're gonna follow rules. When you get your own house, you're gonna have some rules. If people don't follow those rules, there's gonna be some consequences. In society, there are rules, and if you don't follow those rules, there will be consequences."

I realized she was right. My counselor was really working with me. The counselors we had were cool. The stupid consequences and the tickets, they had to do that because that was part of the program. But they would talk to us in a way to make us think about the choices we were making.

One counselor had us write our own obituary as part of our group therapy. Then we read them out loud. I can't remember all I wrote, but it impressed the other inmates. "Wow, Dellenna, that is so good."

But the counselor didn't buy it. "Dellenna, you left out how you would die. You don't seem like the type of person to OD."

She fed right into my ego. I said, "I know, because I can smoke or drink you and whoever else under the table."

But she persisted. "How would you die?"

I thought about that. "You know what, I would be that female that would be found in a ditch somewhere, with my panties down to my ankles, beat up and stabbed, my lighter in one hand and my *stem* in the other in a death grip. That's how you would find me."

And when I said that, I was like *damn.* It was so real to me because people were actually dying like that. Truck drivers used to put me out all the time in the middle of fuckin' nowhere because I wouldn't do something. I can't count how many times I've been beat up, raped, and left for dead.

In this Therapeutic Community, having the counselor ask me about how I would die, thinking about the lighter and the stem, I was like *omigod.* I didn't want to die like that. It was the moment of clarity that jolted me back to reality.

I got on top of my behavior and started following the stupid rules. I worked my way up to accountant, which was the second highest in the hierarchy of service.

I had a lot of admirers in prison. A lot of the gay women tried to get with me. When my counselor found out I had a girlfriend, she said, "Girl, stop playin'. You ain't gay."

"I know, but it's something to do in here."

"Stop playin'. You are not gay for the stay."

"I know, I'm not even having sex."

Both times when I was locked up, even though I was physically locked up, I felt mentally free—free from the obsession of drugs. I did not have crack cocaine controlling my every thought. The first time I was locked up in Plane State, I did use other people's medications and the second time, I abused coffee. You can abuse coffee but doing that was nothing like the obsession and compulsion of crack cocaine.

Free from my obsession, I could think about what I wanted to think about and do what I wanted to do within the rules. I wasn't using in the TC program. It's funny how people find God or get reconnected to God in prison, but once they leave prison, they leave God behind. That's because when they are released, they are not ready to change. I wasn't either.

But while I was in there, I embraced the freedom. With the obsession lifted, I was able to think clearly. I was able to reflect on my life. The letters from my family kept coming and helped me to embrace the freedom. The letters gave me hope that I could change. They reminded me that I was not only loved but worthy of love. Writing to my family was therapeutic and reminded me that I was not alone.

March 10, 2001

Jallanna,

Hey, Baby J, how are you? I'm doing good. Well, you remember when I told you I won't be able to call cuz I won't have a phone? Well, the phone is off so I will have to write you. You can write me too. Actually, I would love that. Please send me more pictures of you and please draw more pictures of us. Send me some cards, too, because I love your stationary. Besides, receiving anything from you will make my week. I saw the prettiest moon the other night. I was wondering if you saw it, too. Well, Baby Doll, I'm gonna go take a shower and I'll be looking forward to hearing from you. I love you big much. Love always,

Mama Dee

March 21, 2001

Jallanna,

Hey, lil J. How are you doing? I'm doing good, in fact I'm doing great because I received 2 letters in the mail from you today. That made my week. Thank you for the pictures you drew and colored for me. They are lovely. You color and draw very good now and your handwriting looks wonderful. You're getting better and better. You are a very smart little girl. Tell Grandma to send me some pictures of you and you keep drawing me pictures. I would really like that. Guess what I saw the other night. A blue moon. It was so pretty. You know I immediately thought of you. I was wondering if you saw it too. I love you, Jallanna. And I miss you big much. I love you big much, too!!

I love you all.

Well, I wanted to let you know I was thinking of you (as always). And you put a smile on my face today with your pictures. That was really nice of you. You put a smile on my face every time I think of you. (BIG SMILE) By the way, how are you doing in school? Oh yeah and have you seen any Angels lately? Cuz I've been sending them to give you a kiss goodnight. Every night. Well, I gotta go. I'll write you again soon. Please send me some pictures of you. Don't 4 get to remind grandma. Kiss grandpa and grandma 4 me. And be good Baby J. I miss you and love you lots.

Love Always,

Mama (Dee)

XXXOXXXO

XXXOXXXO

I give you Baby Kisses

May 2001

Hey Mom.

How ya doing. I'm doing good. I like this program they put me in. I hope you all got my cards I sent you. They keep me busy here and I can't write how I want to. Please when you have time send me Paul's address. Oh yeah did Laraurelle have a boy or a girl? Tell everyone I said Hello. Don't worry about me cuz I'm right where I need to be.

Tell my Daddy I said Hi, Daddy, and I love you. Well, I gotta go, it's late and we get up at 5 a.m. every day; 9:30 on weekends. Imagine that. Believe it or not, Mom, I do get up at 5 a.m. and they don't have to ask me twice. How many times did you have to come back and wake me up? I don't tell them give me 10 more minutes either. I get up. Unbelievable huh. See, I can change.

It's all about acceptance and discipline. And guess what, I have patience like you now. Why didn't I listen to you and my dad. I always gotta learn the hard way. All I know is God's plan is better than mine. Well, I'm going to bed. I love you all and good night.

Love,

Dellenna (Smile Big)

The only perfect child you have (ha ha)

May 2001

Mom,

Hey, How R U doing? I'm doing good. I sent my award home so you can see. I got an award for most positive attitude. Did you get your birthday card? I've been writing y'all at least once a week.

All I want you to do is pray 4 me cuz the rest is up to me. I miss Jallanna and you all so much. And I know that girl didn't name her fish Mrs. Dee. (Smiley face) So when R U gonna get her a cat or dog? (HA HA)

A cat would be easier. Thank you 4 the cards. Thank you 4 everything. Please don't give up on me. Please don't. Tell my dad I said Hello and I love him BIG MUCH. I love you daddy. (Smiley face)

Love,

Dellenna

May 14, 2001

Dear Dellenna,

I wanted to let you know that I received my birthday card you sent the day before my birthday. Thank you so much. It made me feel good to get the card and to know you are safe and doing good.

I read the poem and broke down completely and started crying and could not stop. I truly will never be the same again. It is a wonderful poem and it says too much and has so much truth in it. I will always have it with me.

Dellenna, I am so thankful you are in the drug program and are doing good. No one is perfect and we all make mistakes, but you need to make corrections and keep on going. You can have so much going for you if you only change your ways and believe that God will help you and show you the right way to go. You are so beautiful and very intelligent and will go places. We all miss you and are praying for you.

Jallanna did receive her Easter card and birthday card. She has sent more mail to you and I am sure you will get it before this letter arrives. Thank you again for my birthday card and the poem.

Love,
Mom

Aug. 4, 2001

Jallanna,

Hey baby girl, how are you doing? I saw the prettiest full moon last night. I immediately thought of you. A beautiful moon for my beautiful daughter. I heard you went fishing and caught a big fish, the biggest fish. Well, I should be seeing you at the end of the month. I miss you. I can't wait to hold you and give you a big kiss. Did Grandpa tell you I called? You and Grandma wasn't there. So I just talked to him. Girl you stay gone. I heard you had a busy summer. I can't wait to see you. Hey, I need you to do something for me, I need you to give my big brother (Paul) a BIG hug and kiss for me. I love you and will see you soon.

Love,
Dee (Mama)
P.S. Look to the moon.

My family is awesome and so supportive. I am very blessed and grateful. There were many other letters from many other family members. They really helped the time go by faster by sending me letters and pictures. And they supported me by sending money on a regular basis. People do not understand that when you have a family member doing time, the entire family is doing time with the person behind bars. I understood that at that time.

That understanding motivated me to work on myself. The assignments the counselors gave us were helpful and thought-provoking. They helped me to both identify and label my feelings. In order for me to heal, I had to sort through my past. I had to let all the bad go to make room for the healing to begin.

While I was in prison, the counselors had us write about our previous behavior, the consequences, how we felt, etc. I wrote about things like the time my mother had my brother arrest me at church; how I stole money from my parents and took their cars in the middle of the night to get high; how I disappeared after my first time in prison and went back to Clinton Park rather than go home with my parents and Jallanna; and about the intervention my family did in Minnesota. I wrote about how prostitution made me feel.

Me prostituting my body makes me feel ashamed. All the immoral things I did to get dope made me feel useless and unworthy. Hearing people talk bad about me when I walked down the street and the names they called me because of all the things I did to get money or dope made me feel worthless and stupid. How I put myself out there made me feel humiliated, guilty and hurt. I didn't care what I did, who I did it with, or who saw me do it, as long as I was getting high and that made me feel dirty, nasty and very low down.

I also wrote *I know all my family loves me and supports me but I got to love myself. I'm tired of letting myself and my loved ones down. I've taken and taken from my family and myself and this is my chance to give back.*

One assignment was to write 50 consequences of my behavior.

Here are some of them.

Due to my addiction, I became a compulsive liar. I felt fake, bad and foolish.

Due to my addiction, I missed the most important years of my daughter's life. I had no time for her. I felt cheated, uninvolved and irresponsible.

Due to my addiction, I have been in and out of treatment several times. I felt stupid, hopeless, defeated and foolish.

Due to my addiction, I lost the trust of family and friends. I felt lonely, responsible, powerless, rejected and shut out.

Due to my addiction, I had sex w/people I did not know. I felt disgusted, dirty, no good and nasty.

Due to my addiction, I have no dreams. I feel hopeless and inferior.

Due to my addiction, I have to start all over. I feel scared, hurt and angry.

Due to my addiction I lost Dellenna, I lost my self-respect, my dignity, and had no integrity or self-esteem whatsoever. I felt worthless and low down.

After my second stay in prison, I was able to actually take some positive things away with me that I didn't leave in prison, like I'd done in the past. I learned how important it was to follow rules, and I learned that I didn't want to die an addict. I felt like I could start with a clean slate when I got back to Minnesota.

But I still had a yearning to feel like I was accepted and belonged. I didn't understand, at the time, the connection between my thinking, my behaviors, and the disease of addiction. I also didn't understand the importance of changing my surroundings—people, places, and things—to stay clean. I thought when counselors told me that I had to change people, places, and things, it didn't mean my family. Hanging with certain family members who were still *in the lifestyle* was not conducive to my recovery. But I didn't get that, not until long after I got out of prison.

5

Minnesota repeat

My life for the next two years is kind of a blur. I know my parents picked me up from the prison and drove me back to Minnesota, but I don't remember it. I stayed with them and Jallanna in Cottage Grove for a while. I knew I had to change "people, places, and things" in order to stay clean, but I didn't understand that changing "people" also meant family, which was very difficult for me. Some of my brothers and sisters and cousins were still smokin' and gettin' high. Being around them wasn't good for my recovery. At some point, I started hanging out with members of my family who were in the lifestyle. They did drugs or sold drugs, and I started using again. I started with the marijuana, then it progressed to crack and heroin.

Addiction is a powerful force; it consumed me. I understand today that I used to numb myself. I did not want to feel. I did not want to feel that I did not belong. I did not want to feel the hatred that I had for Dellenna. I did not want to feel the shame and guilt for the things I did before and during the drug use—not to mention the shame of how I turned my back on my family, my daughter, and myself. The things I did to get my drugs were shameful as well. The drugs were a way to cope with those feelings. I would get high, feel numb, then as I was coming down, the feelings and thoughts would return and intensify. In order for me not to feel, I would get high again. So I would do some shameful shit to get drugs to get high to feel numb, only to come down from the drugs and be even more miserable than I was before. Hence, the vicious cycle.

Active addiction is centered around getting drugs, using drugs, and finding ways and means to get more drugs. That is all I thought about. When the obsession became overpowering, I acted compulsively. I did not think about anyone or anything but getting high and what I had to do to get high. That is the self-centeredness. Obsession, compulsion, and self-centeredness are the three ingredients that birth addiction. When I was in that state of mind, I destroyed anything in the way of getting high, including my family and me. No one hurt me like I hurt myself. I put myself in harm's way many times to get high "one more time."

One time a man broke my arm trying to take my drugs. He picked me up and slammed me down on my elbow. If he only knew what I had to do to get those drugs! I was not giving that shit up nor was I sharing. I didn't go to the hospital until three or four days later. I had all this crack and was smoking it with one arm, and people were telling me, "You need to go to the hospital," and I told them, "I will when this crack is gone." Once the crack was gone, I turned a few tricks even with my arm broken. I finally ended up going to North Memorial Hospital.

While in the emergency department, I went in and out of the bathroom to smoke the crack that I had copped before going in there. The doctor set my elbow and put pins in it. I thought to myself, *Fuck the break! I need help for my drug problem.* I told the nurse, "I'm not leaving until you give me help for my drug problem." I thought they weren't going to help me, so then I told them, "I will kill you and everyone else in here and myself if you don't help me." That's what I had to say in order to get help. I ended up in yet another psych ward.

From the psych ward, I was transferred to an inpatient treatment program at Unity. In every program, I picked up information. I always took it in but didn't apply it until I was ready. I've been in quite a few programs, too many to count, and in all the programs, they teach the same information. I never forgot the information. It was like I put it on a shelf in my head because I knew I would need it one day if I survived the wilderness. I had to make sure I survived to see the day when I would be able to use the information that would help me to change, the day when I no longer had the desire to use drugs, the day I was ready to do something different.

Journaling was a coping mechanism I picked up in one of the programs. It was effective for me. It helped me to process not only my feelings but also my thoughts and day-to-day life. I started a journal atNorth Memorial, and the first entry is about a dream I had.

July 9, 2002

In the dream, I was at my cousin Lynn's house. I wasn't actually using in the dream but I knew I was in active addiction. My dad came in and he was using crack. I didn't see him smoke in my dream but I knew he was using. I could tell by his appearance. He came in and he was hungry. He reached in front of me and grabbed the shrimp that was in front of me. His appearance made me feel hurt, gloomy, troubled, sad, disturbed, afraid, wounded, sorrowful, crushed, miserable, humbled. I wanted to reach out to him. His skin was bad looking. I felt hurt, sad, and sorrowful. For some reason, when he was leaving, he thought I was leaving, too (possibly going to use). I remember he had his work pants on, and he had a bunch of quarters in a container attached to his belt. I wasn't thinking about using w/ the money. I remember thinking, "He's not using like I use because he still has money." But I remember feeling really bad when I saw his appearance.

He walked over to me and pulled my hood over my head and as he was tying my tie, he told me "Everything is going to be all right. Everything is going to be OK." I told him, "Dad, I'm not leaving. I'm staying here!" I remember feeling a sense of relief. I also remember a peaceful feeling. I think God (my Father) is telling me I'll be all right. Thank you, Jesus. Thank you 4 being U. Thank you for caring through my addiction, thank you for letting me live again. Thank you for giving me my life back. Thank you for my recovery.

I always had dreams that would give me hints about the future.

I have dreams like that to this day. I believe strongly that my dreams are messages about my life.

From the inpatient program, I went to the Hart House, a transitional housing program for women in recovery in St. Paul. I continued to write in my journal. For the entry dated Friday, July 19, 2002, I wrote Jeremiah 31:17 in the margin. That verse says, "There is hope for your future," declares the Lord, "and your children will return to their own territory.

Next to that notation I wrote: *I got a message from God today. He told me there is hope for my future… As long as I keep doing what I'm doing. I got discharged from Unity today and I arrived at Hart House today safely. I spent the day with my Mom and Jallanna. I went to (the doctor). Jallanna is silly. She is so loveable. My sponsor Pamala is out of town. When I got here, I was bored so I met a peer and went to a recovery meeting. I loved it. I got my 30 days key chain today. I stayed clean today cuz I chose to. It felt good. Today I feel proud, determined, hopeful, happy, encouraged, marvelous, grateful, alive, peaceful, confident, courageous, independent, brave, and anxious to C what God has planned for tomorrow. It's all about the choices I make. I love myself today. I love Jallanna every day.*

At the Hart House, I was able to get out to see my parents and Jallanna more. I had freedom. I could come and go as I pleased, which eventually got me into trouble. I continued to write in my journal every day.

July 20, 2002

Today was a beautiful day. Me and my mom, Peggy and Rita all went for breakfast at Perkins. We were supposed to go to Rhondo Days Parade, but it was raining so we went to see Men in Black II. Then we went to Granny's house…I saw Chanel, Brandi, Maceo, and a lot of other people. I had fun clean…Then my Mom dropped me off. Today, I felt giggly, loved, trusted, enthusiastic, courageous, determined, proud, excited, cheerful and full of joy. Also grateful, confident that God would take the rain away and also I would stay clean. I was at peace today and very pleased. I love myself today and I love Jallanna every day. I thought about her when I saw the moon. Daisy also took me shopping for underclothes. I love my Mom and Dad. They R so supportive.

July 21, 2002

I spent the day with my mom. We went to Rhondo Days. She bought me a belt and some Chanel sunglasses. They are cute. We went grocery shopping and then back to the house. She cooked and I got my clothes. I watched TV. We went and got Jallanna. She was camping with the Girl Scouts. I know she had fun even though she said she was bored. She is so silly…We went home and ate. Then they dropped me off. I unpacked and put all my clothes away. We had our first group tonight. We had to say 3 things we are grateful for. And choose a word in the bag and say what it means to us. My word was "compassion". Overall today was a relaxing but busy day. I enjoyed being with my mom and Jallanna. I need to love myself more. But I love Jallanna every day. Lord, help me with my feelings of jealousy and inadequacy. Help me to be OK with who I am. In the name of Jesus, I pray. Amen.

In the margin of the page, I wrote: *I miss Paul, my dad, and Kahala.*

With the freedom that I had at the Hart House, I was out and about. One of the things I learned early on is that just because I stopped using, that does not mean others did and they will try to get me dirty before I can help them to get clean. I was new in recovery. I was vulnerable. My foundation in my recovery was shaky—if I had a foundation at all. I was only at Hart House a few days before I was offered drugs.

July 22, 2002

Today was not an exciting day but it was beautiful. I went window shopping and on my way to Maceo's house, I walked through the "zone". Somebody stopped and offered me some crack. I said, "NO, I don't get high no more." I was proud of myself today. I went to Attack Graphics and got my bag and helped the owner out with a couple things and he paid me. Thank God. Then I went to a recovery meeting. The reading was about being spiritually dead. Then we read from the recovery book. I also went to the business meeting. Overall, I had a blessed day today…Thank you, Lord, for keeping me clean today and giving me strength in my time of weakness.

July 23, 2002

God is leading my life.

I am just where I need to be. Today God sent me my sponsor. I finally met Pam today. She is lovely. She showed me her art studio (her soul). She is so talented. We connected. Thank you, God, I need to shut up and listen more. I went to a meeting with her today. Then we went for coffee. I loved it. I also got my AIDS test results. "Negative." Thank you, Jesus…I love being clean. I love myself today. I love Jallanna every day. The moon is pretty. Today I feel blessed to have Pam. I felt proud, determined, confident, joy, understood, grateful, alive, fulfilled, peaceful, encouraged and valued…Thank you, Jesus, for keeping me sober.

At this time in my recovery, I struggled with craving for attention from the opposite sex. I needed validation from men as I was in a place where I was unable to validate myself. I wasn't there yet. I had a spiritual void, an emptiness, that on many occasions I attempted to fill with flesh. The void came when the drugs were removed from my life. The drugs served a purpose; they validated me. They helped me to feel like I belonged or like I was a part of something. They made me feel accepted. When the drugs were taken out of the equation, I was left with a big void that I tried filling with anything and everything. At this moment in my life, it happened to be men. I confused sex with love, and I got into relationships for all the wrong reasons. This was the beginning of another bottom.

My journal during this time often references men that I met—P., June, and others. My sponsor was telling me that I should not get into any relationships but instead focus on my recovery. I found that difficult and unrealistic.

July 26, 2002

Follow Through

I missed you yesterday! I slipped yesterday! I woke up, did not pray, did not do my morning readings and ended up making bad choices. Today I had sex. I think I like him but I want to take things slow. I talked with sponsor today. She told me no relationships for a year, do 90 and 90 and gave me my 4th step—(Make a searching and fearless moral inventory of ourselves). I feel confused about P. I want to get to know myself but it's hard cuz I like him. I like the way he makes me feel. He's got a good heart but I'm confused. Today I went to a baseball game that was fun. I enjoy myself with P. and Lonnie. I talked to Lonnie today. He told me to protect my heart. Today I feel better than yesterday. Even though I slipped up, I'm still determined. I think I need to talk more with Pam. I don't want to keep shit from her. I want to stay clean… I still got a long way to go. Help me, Lord. U lead and I will follow.

During my stay at the Hart House, someone mentioned a support group for women recovering from prostitution. I was in denial about my issues stemming from prostitution but I thought I'd check it out. What I did not understand, but learned many years later, was that dealing with all those men while in my recovery, getting my needs met (emotionally, physically, and mentally) by them was prostitution, and it was also a form of me using. I actually substituted men for the drugs.

Aug. 8, 2002

I forgot to write U yesterday. I think I was just tired. I went to Breaking Free yesterday (intake). And I went to recovery meeting at Midway at 12:30 p.m. I will go to a meeting on Tuesday at Breaking Free for prostitution. I hooked up with June and did the thang. Found out Jallanna stole some Gameboy games. That made me sad. It upset me and I was disappointed in my baby girl.

Although this was the beginning of yet another bottom, I was attempting to do the right thing. I honestly thought I was in a good space. I did not realize the connection between my behaviors with these men and the disease of addiction. I did not understand I was playing with fire. I guess that is why denial stands for Don't Even Know I Am Lying to myself. I continued to work my program or so I thought. I didn't realize I was working towards a relapse.

I never forgot where my help and strength came from. I always asked for God's help so I could stay clean, but I failed to do my part. I kept hanging around family members who were not healthy for me during my early recovery. They drank alcohol and smoked weed. I had no business hanging around them when I was trying to stay clean. Here are some excerpts from my journal:

Aug. 14, 2002

Thank U Lord for helping me when I was thinking bad. Thank u. I was thinking about using but I talked to you instead. Thank you for being there. I can depend on you. Thank U for my life and my child.

Sept. 4, 2002

Lord, my cousin T. got drunk today. So drunk it wasn't funny but I was laughing out loud and I was hurting inside. I see her pain but her drinking isn't helping. That girl can drink. She was so drunk. I don't like the path she's taking. Lord, help me help her. Help me help me. I don't want to go back to where I was. I'm being stupid. Lord, Help me.

Sept. 23, 2002

Thank you, Lord for another blessed day. Today my morning went good. I went to DJ's and talked to him, then I went to my recovery meeting. Then I went to Tiff's (my close friend Tiffany). We watched movies and I hooked up w/Dan. He's turning himself in tomorrow (so he say). Today I should've went to the 7 p.m. recovery meeting. I'm fucking up going to Tiff's. Lord, help me stay in this house and help me get a grip. Help me slow down. Help me use my head. Thank you for keeping me away from crack. Thank U for my life back. Thank you for Jallanna. Thank you for being you. Thank you for loving me. I feel guilty cuz I'm slowly fucking up. Please forgive me for my sins. I'm quite sure I lied today. Thank you, Jesus, thank you. Love you.

Oct. 2 and 3, 2002

Lord, thank u for that situation. It's all about my choices. Thank U for bringing me back. Thank you. Please forgive me for my sins. I've lied, and I stole, Lord. Please continue to help me. I have faith in you, Lord. Thank you for keep-

ing me clean today. Thank you, Jesus. Help me to follow through. Help me to listen to you. Help me make right choices. I felt grateful I made it back, but I feel troubled, tense, guilty, shame, upset with myself, vulnerable, resentful, disgusted, pissed off, humiliated, ashamed, disgraced, empty, miserable. It all happened so fast. I hooked up with Richard and we went to a bar. I had some money so we played pool. I really fucked up fucking with him. All these emotions were coming. My stomach had butterflies. I had $ and I wanted to see my old friend. Well I saw the white bitch (crack) all right. She got me again. That bitch. She think she got me but I made my ass to a meeting today. No matter what I will keep coming back. After fucking with Richard I saw that bitch again. I could not sleep. Head hurting, hungry, guilty, shame, let down. But now that bitch teaches me something when I'm with her but I learn more w/o her. I can't fuck w/that bitch. She scares me. I can't handle her. She does me bad every time I fuck w/her. Help me, Jesus. I have faith you will help me help myself w/disciplining myself. Thank you, for Jallanna, Tiff and T., gotta watch over them and kids. Thank you for my life back. Thank you for loving me and helping me. Thank you for being you. Thank you. I love you.

I ended up leaving the Hart House because I was still prostituting—not standing on the corner—but I was using people for their money. That behavior led me to use, and eventually I didn't go back there. I also sought treatment at another facility for women called Progress Valley Treatment Center near the Mall of America.

While I was there, I had to take a personality test called the Minnesota Multiphasic Personality Inventory. I think results were accurate for me. One of the counselors told me, "Dellenna, you're the type of person that likes to go over the rules, under the rules, around the rules, bend the rules, anything but flat out break the rules. I don't know if you're serious about recovery." I wasn't. She read me like a book. I thought, *Fuck this lady.* But she was absolutely right.

At Progress Valley, we were required to get a job. I went to the Mall supposedly to find a job, but instead I was hustling on the pool table. Another resident from Progress Valley saw me and told on me, but I lied and said it wasn't me. I wasn't trying to get a job;

I was trying to get high. At Progress Valley, we went on a group outing to a place called Sex World. While the other women were in there, I found a guy who sold me drugs. I brought the drugs back to Progress Valley. I was assigned to clean the bathroom, so I was in there getting high, and for some reason I got the bright idea to do a really clean bathroom. I mixed some ammonia and bleach together. I think the only reason I didn't pass out was because I was high.

After that, the people who ran the house told me they needed a house meeting about me, and I could leave or I could face the house meeting. I knew I was doing wrong, but I thought, "Fuck you, guys. I ain't got time for this; I'm not talking to them about my damn behavior. If they don't want me here, then I'll leave." They did want me to stay but if I wasn't following the rules, then yeah, I had to go. "I'm going to leave if they're going to put me out." I don't think they would have put me out if I had come to the meeting. If I had acknowledged my part, they would have given me another chance, I think. But I was like, "I'll get you before you get me. I'll hurt me before you hurt me."

I had moments where a part of me wanted help but a part of me didn't want help. I didn't really understand the connection between that behavior and my addiction. I thought the addiction was the drugs. I didn't understand that using the drugs is only one symptom. My behavior is another symptom. The way I think is my disease. I didn't understand all of that. I didn't understand that if I continued these behaviors, I would go back to drugs. I thought the drugs were my problem, and if I stopped using drugs, I'd be OK. I've learned that when you take the drugs away, you have a whole lot of other stuff you have to deal with.

When Progress Valley kicked me out, I called a drug dealer I knew to come pick me up. I stayed with him for a bit in south Minneapolis. I eventually ended up going back out on the streets and made my way over to North Minneapolis where I continued to use. Occasionally, I called my mom to check in.

"Dellenna, there's a bed over here at this place. Go check yourself in."

"Mom, I'm tired of getting your hopes up, and getting my hopes up only to let you guys down. Just pray for me. I'm tired of letting everyone down. Just pray that I survive. I gotta get it out of my system. Just pray that I live."

That was the hardest thing I ever had to say to my mom, but I was being honest with myself. I thought, "I'm not going back into treatment and waste some good get-high time."

One time I was standing on a corner prostituting and this black Cadillac pulled up. I jumped in, thinking it was a trick, but it was my mom and dad. Jallanna popped up in the back seat saying "Hi, Mommy." I felt so much shame. They asked me what I was doing. Of course I lied, but they knew. They were on their way home from a relative's house around the corner. I don't even remember how I got out of the car.

I went home to Cottage Grove periodically, when my mom allowed me to. I'd stay for a few days and rest up. Jallanna would be so happy to see me and try to spend time with me, but I was always too tired after being up for weeks at a time. One time I had my mother drop me off back in Minneapolis. Before I got out of the car, I asked her for some money. She scraped up some dollars and change. She asked me where I was going. I answered: "You can drop me off on this corner right here."

"What?"

I repeated, "on this corner, right here." I wanted to prostitute so I could get me some drugs.

She did what I asked. Later, I found out she pulled the car around the corner and cried and cried. She knew what I was doing and it hurt her to the core.

Once again, I was consumed with the lifestyle: living to use and using to live. I was back to turning tricks again. I never had a pimp. I was more of a renegade. I wasn't going to do all this and then give my money to someone.

When I turned a trick, I learned the hard way to get my money first. I had little hidden pockets in my coat because tricks often tried to take the money back. One time I was with this guy in his car in an alley and he gave me some money for some head. I hid it in my coat. Then, while I was in the middle of giving him a blowjob, he wanted to make another deal. I thought to myself: *I do not want to stop and get the money only to start all over again. I will be here all day.* So I decided I'll get the money afterwards. When I finished, I said, "Can I get the rest of the money?" He said, "Do you have change? Give me the money you got because I don't have any change." I said, "You said you'd take me to McDonalds. You can get some change there." I thought, *I'm not bringing this money back out.*

I could tell something wasn't right. He pulled out a roll of twenties, and he looked over at me and said, "Give me the money." Suddenly his fist was coming toward me.

Now I'm not a Bible-thumping, scripture-quoting person. However, I was raised in church; I do believe in God and I have trust in His Word. I don't know what came out of me, but I know my spirit interceded. Out of nowhere, I started quoting, actually yelling, Bible scripture. "In the name of Jesus Christ, Satan, I rebuke you. No weapon formed against me shall prosper." And I was saying it really loud, from my heart, over and over again. His fist was in my face jerking back and forth like he was trying to hit me but he couldn't—almost like there was an invisible force field stopping him. I believe that with all my heart.

As I continued to yell scripture, I looked him in his eyes. His eyes were all black. I was making eye contact and yelling, "In the name of Jesus Christ, I rebuke you." Somehow, I maneuvered my way out of the car. I landed on my knees, and he sped off. I stayed on my knees praying. "Thank you, God. Thank you, God. Thank you."

I never lost my faith when I was out there. I knew I was in the wilderness. I left God; He never left me. It irritates me when people say God doesn't listen to a sinner's prayer because there have been so many times when He heard me, so many times when He saved me. Even though I was sinning at the time, I know He heard me. There's no other reason I'm here had it not been for prayer—my prayers, and the prayers of the prayer warriors in my family who were praying for me.

I was on the ground in the alley. A woman was walking to her car parked in the alley behind her house. I asked, "Ma'am, can I please use your phone?" She said, "You're a prostitute." I asked again, "Ma'am, would you please call 911?" She hesitated, and I asked for the third time, "Can you please call 911?" Finally, she called 911. Before she walked away, she said to me, "You filthy whore" and some other stuff. When the police got there, I told them what had happened. A female officer said, "But you're a prostitute." I said, "Ma'am, I don't care what I am, that man's dangerous and you need to stop him before he hurts someone else." They laughed at me.

When you're a prostitute and you get assaulted, nobody cares because you're a prostitute and they think you deserve it. You're not a human being. It was a blow to my self-esteem the way society was looking at me. Instead of helping me, they laughed at me because of my lifestyle, because of the choices I was making, or rather, the choices the drugs were making for me. Because I was doing what I was doing, they did not see a human being; they saw a crackhead whore. I can't count how many times I've been beat up, raped, and left for dead, and had tried to get help from some police. They're like "But you're a prostitute." But I'm a human. I believe that I should be able to walk down the street buck naked and nobody has the right to put their hands on me.

There's a gray area with sexual assault when it comes to prostitution. Today I speak on a lot of panels about sexual assault and human trafficking even though I was never trafficked. These women are prostitutes against their will. They are being sold and some of them are under the influence. The trafficker keeps them under the influence so they will be dependent on them for their drugs.

It's sad, the double standard of the police. Didn't they take an oath to protect and serve me, regardless of the lifestyle that I was living?

There are a lot of good police officers like my brother Paul; a lot of them have helped me. But on the day that I was in that alley, those officers made me feel like shit. Needless to say, I went and got high because I didn't like the way I felt when I allowed the men to do things to me, things that I never thought I'd do. I used drugs to mask feeling dirty and guilty and ashamed. Then when the drugs were all gone, I had to get more, so I had to go do the dirty act again. To stop feeling those feelings, I'd use.

As my disease progressed, I was in dangerous situations more and more.

One time, a woman in Minneapolis tried to fight me. I don't like to fight and I was scared, but she had an audience so we were fightin' in the middle of the street. She didn't know how scared I was. Somehow, I got a wrestling move on her, and I got on top of her. I had her pinned down and she could not move.

She started yelling, "Get her off me, get her off me." One of the guys watching pulled me off her.

Everyone watching was like "Ok, she can fight, she can hold her own," referring to me. That woman never put her hands on me or talked shit to me again. Neither did the others. I did not like to fight, and I tried to avoid fights, but I would defend myself.

Another time a woman hit me from behind. In the midst of my anger and fear, I turned around and we started fighting. She was able to get on top of me. I had a sharp object in my hand—I don't remember what—and I poked it into her neck. Something inside me screamed, "Don't hurt her. Just jab it in her neck hard enough to get her up off you." That's what I did. She got off me and that was that.

When I told that story to a guy in North Minneapolis, he said, "There's something different about you. You don't belong out here." I remembered that the drug dealer in Texas who wanted to take me to rehab had told me the same thing.

I never messed with people nor did I start fights, but if you started with me, I talked shit or defended myself. One time I had a fight with this girl and the next day, I saw that she was hungry. I had money so I bought her something to eat. My mother always told me, "If someone's hungry, I don't care who they are, you feed them." I did that. No matter the situation, I still had a heart.

I had moments like that—like when I helped that old woman who was an invalid in Texas. In St. Paul there was a little girl about 8 years old who lived at a drug house where I used. One morning, no one would take her to school. I thought to myself, *She has got to get out of the house; this is not healthy for her. The school is a better place for her to be.* So that day I walked her to school. It was about a 45-minute walk, and we talked the whole way. She was a sweet little girl. I thought to myself, *I am doing this for a child I barely know, and I don't even do this for my own child.*

Although I still had a heart and I sincerely cared about people, on many occasions, I did cause harm to people. Living the drug lifestyle, you cannot be soft, or people will take advantage of you. Not only did the drugs change my personality but the lifestyle did as well. It's like do or die, survival of the fittest. Both the drugs and the lifestyle will bring the worst out of a person.

Throughout active addiction I experienced and witnessed so much violence. It comes with the lifestyle. When you're out there on the street, it is no joke. Nothing surprised me. I may have been desensitized from the drugs. I remember one time a woman told me she had just got raped. I felt for her because that happened to me multiple times. I told her, "If you continue to live this lifestyle, it won't be the last time that happens. So either accept it or stop what you're doing." Then I shared my drugs with her because she had none and was in no condition to make money to get some. I have experienced all kinds of crazy stuff out there. My smart mouth and bad attitude didn't help matters either.

While I was in Minneapolis, I went to houses where I could buy drugs and smoke if I paid the person who lived in the house. I only had to give them some money or drugs. Sometimes I didn't like the drugs that were being sold or I didn't like how disrespectful the dealers were towards me, so I bought drugs elsewhere and brought them to one of the other drug houses. I paid the person who lived there so I could stay and smoke the drugs I got somewhere else. The drug dealers in the house did not like that. One time a dealer got real mad because I was not buying drugs from them. He told me, "You can't come over here, and you need to leave with that shit. If you don't, I'm gonna hit you with that two-by-four."

"Go ahead."

"I'm going to count to four: one, two..."

As he finished counting "three, four" I pulled a screwdriver out of my purse.

He tried to hit me in the head with the two-by-four but I turned away and he got my shoulder. I swung at him with the screwdriver and I stabbed him. I kept stabbing him, and he started to bleed. His two friends jumped in because I was really getting him good. They started kicking me and hitting me. I tried to keep swinging. I was just protecting myself. I didn't start shit but I wasn't going to let him put me out of the house. When they finished, I was hurt real bad. I couldn't get up so I crawled to the back room. Because I was high, I did not feel the pain. I wanted to get higher, so I sent someone out to get drugs from somewhere else and bring them back.

Another time this man beat me and tried to rape me in my ass. Thank God I got away. I don't remember how, but I got away. I don't even remember what I was feeling. I imagine I felt dirty, low, beaten, like I wanted to just crawl in a hole and die. I felt so alone and all I wanted to do was get high.

After that, I left Minneapolis and made my way over to St. Paul and continued to use there. I was getting high in the house where the little girl lived, the one I had walked to school. I got into it with the dealer. He said something to me, and me with my smart mouth, said something back, and he knocked the shit out of me. I stopped buying drugs from him for a while. Mind you, if I was desperate, I'd have bought drugs from him.

I was very stubborn. I'm surprised that I'm still alive. But a few days later, the guy who hit me picked me up and told me he wanted to apologize. But he wasn't sincere. He had motives. He made a deal with me about some trick he wanted me to meet. He said we'd get some money. I got his ass back. I met up with the trick and took all the money.

I was always doing crazy shit to get back at people. I could not beat them physically, so I got revenge by fucking with their heads or getting in their pockets—meaning, somehow messing with their money.

It got to the point where people weren't letting me in the house even if I had money and drugs because I was so crazy. Usually when your drugs are gone, you gotta go. You're not useful anymore. But they weren't letting me into the house at all.

In St. Paul there was a motel where people got high. There was no electricity; even the people who owned the hotel were smoking crack. One time I went there when I felt so tired after being up for a week. Something had happened to me and I don't remember what, but I know it was bad. Maybe someone tried to rape me. I was feeling scared and ashamed. *I am so tired of this shit, I have got to stop,* I thought. Everybody was smoking, but nobody was trickin' so I couldn't make any money. But God was always watching over me. A guy that worked there unlocked a room so I could sleep. "You'll be safe here." The next day, I woke up and left.

I eventually found an abandoned car to get high in. It was the end of November, after Thanksgiving Day when I'd seen Jallanna at my grandmother's house. Winter was starting and it was really cold. I had been up for days with no sleep. I kept telling myself, *I'm gonna catch a date and go get a hotel room,* but every little bit of money I got went to buy drugs. Then I'd go to the abandoned car to smoke. One day I was standing on University near Dale Street, and this big truck slowed down, pulled over, and eventually stopped. When I saw big trucks, I saw dollar signs! I ran to the truck and got in. Then the driver told me that he's only got $5.

"What about your EFS checks? I know you got more money."

"How do you know about that?"

"I used to travel with truck drivers. I know you got a way to get some cash."

"Nope, not tonight."

Whatever. I was so tired. I turned the trick with him for $5 and fell asleep in the back of his truck. I was in a "crack coma"— that's what we call a hard sleep. I had been up for damn near a week. The next morning, he woke me up and bought me a McGriddle from McDonalds. He said, "Where do you want me to drop you off? Or you can come with me, and I'll take care of you."

All I heard was "I'll take care of you."

I answered, "Let's roll."

6

A prayer answered

We head out on the road, and I find out L.T. is in recovery with twelve years clean. Yet he was trickin'. The disease of addiction can manifest itself in many ways. Even if someone has some clean time, it doesn't mean they aren't acting out in another area. He was at a very low point in his life.

Because L.T. was feeding and clothing me, I felt obligated to have sex with him. That was the only thing I had to offer. I found a book on the twelve-step program in the truck cab. Of course, I was already familiar with the program. I read the book and he talked to me about it. But he didn't want to hear anything I had to say because in his eyes I was a newcomer. I wasn't a newcomer; I was familiar with the program but wasn't ready to stop using. I kept the information on a shelf in my head.

I challenged L.T. and he didn't like that. Some people think it's not proper for newcomers to challenge the more experienced members. I think that's a bunch of bullshit. To this day, I learn by both listening to and challenging the more experienced members. And I learn from the newcomers. I learn from people who are still using. You never know where help is going to come from; you have to stay open-minded.

I developed a daily routine in L.T.'s truck. I woke up in the morning, cleaned the cab, and did my meditation. I noticed L.T. was always on the phone with other recovering addicts. Although he was on the road, he stayed connected to people in recovery, including a woman that I asked to be my sponsor before we got to Rochester, New York, where L.T lived. She gave me assignments to do. I hadn't met her, but we were building a relationship via phone.

We arrived in Rochester on Dec. 24, 2003, a Wednesday. It was 50 degrees, which was warm for that time of year. L.T. told me I could stay at his apartment with him, but I could not have a house key, and he was not going to let me drive his cars. I'm thinking, *What the fuck? I'm not going to be a prisoner. I'm gonna be in the house all day?*

I began thinking this is the worst mistake I've ever made. We started arguing Christmas morning, our first morning after arriving in Rochester. We ended up going to a twelve-step meeting. I shared that I was brand new to Rochester and New York state and that I had less than thirty days clean and I felt like using. Several of the men at the meeting hugged me but not one woman. *Here we go with this bullshit—these bitchy ass women.*

We celebrated Christmas at my sponsor's house. I told her I didn't want to stay with L.T. She said, "Ok, baby, this is what you're gonna do." She told me to have L.T. take me to the Department of Human Services, tell them I am homeless, and ask for cash assistance, food stamps, and emergency housing so I could get my own apartment.

When I told L.T. about my plan, he said, "God brought you to my life to be my wife."

I shot back: "I have a connection with God, too, and He didn't tell me shit. You need to take me to the fuckin' shelter."

The day after Christmas, we went to DHS. The clerk asked me, "Where did you stay last night? Did you stay at the Cadillac?" I didn't know the Cadillac was a seedy hotel for transients but fortunately I said yes, and she said, "We're gonna place you at The Salvation Army Hope House." If I had told her about staying at L.T.'s apartment, I would not have been considered homeless and wouldn't have received the emergency housing. Ironically, sleeping on someone's couch is not considered being homeless.

L.T. reluctantly dropped me off at Hope House that day, but he continued to bring me money and some things I needed. I wanted to get away from him but needed the money. I continued going to twelve-step meetings. There were a lot of good people at Hope House. Some are still my friends to this day. Miss Love was the director there, and a woman named Tracey worked there. They were really nice. Lisa, a woman who lived there, took me under her wing and taught me how to catch the buses. I wasn't from Rochester so didn't know the city. Every day I sat at a table at Hope House and looked through the classified ads for apartments. I yelled out a street name and people told me if it was a bad neighborhood or a good one.

On Jan. 14, 2004 I moved into my own apartment on Ambrose Street, supposedly the good end of Ambrose, which I found out was only two blocks long. It was a cool studio apartment. I had an antique tub in my bathroom, and I love antique tubs. That pretty much sold me—plus the walk-in closet. I'm thinking, *This is the freakin' bomb.* But even with DHS paying the rent, I did not have enough money for necessities.

I started going to Evelyn Brandon Health Center, an outpatient program for chemical dependency and mental health on Lake Avenue, about a block from my apartment. I walked through the alley and it was right there. My first home group was at this little church off Lyell Avenue near Austin. I was committed to attending my meetings there once a week. Soon I chaired the twelve-step meetings, made the coffee, did service work. It made me feel a part of something. One day they tried to give me the keys to open the doors, and I said, "I don't want the keys. I'm not ready for that."

Two other recovering addicts walked with me to my home group every Tuesday. Lyell is not a street you want to walk down by yourself, being early in recovery. Since I was not from Rochester and had moved into the neighborhood, I did not know about Lyell till later.

I was only getting $17 a month from DHS and needed more

to live on. I was used to taking care of myself. I didn't want to ask people to help me because then I felt obligated, and I hated that sense of obligation. Instead of humbling myself and asking for help, I played games to get people to offer me what I wanted or needed. Who was offering me stuff?

Men.

One guy who worked for the city of Rochester drove to my apartment in a city vehicle, gave me money, took me to get my nails done—stuff like that. He said God told him to help me and not have sex with me. I thought, *OK.* I told him I needed a microwave oven, some furniture and this, that, and this. He took me shopping and bought the stuff I needed. After he brought it up to my apartment, he tried to make a move.

"No, you said God told you not to have sex with me. You don't want to go against God! You don't play with God because that's what God told you to do. That's what you said God said." I kept saying that as I escorted him out the door. He often came by and knocked on the door. I wouldn't even undo the chain lock when I opened the door. He passed the money to me. I knew he was a big trick. I also knew I could get what I needed from him without giving him any sex, which made him want me more, and then he'd do more for me.

Those are the kinds of games that I played with people. I didn't realize at the time that that's hurtful. I didn't care because I was getting my needs met. In my mind today, I see that as prostitution. Although we didn't have sex, I was using him and compromising my morals and my values. Any time I compromise my morals and my values, that's prostitution. I didn't have many morals and values at that time. I used a lot of people to furnish my apartment, and some agencies also helped me.

I remember someone in a recovery meeting telling me that I can do anything I want when I am clean—just don't use. I later found out that was a lie. There are some things that I absolutely cannot do in recovery. I needed money and the way I knew how to get it was to start doing tricks again. Although I was technically clean, I was playing with fire with my thinking and my behaviors.

The lifestyle can sometimes be more addictive than the drugs themselves. I couldn't be humble and patient and wait for things to come. I wanted what I wanted now. I got what I wanted the wrong way. Quitting drugs is one thing but the lifestyle is a whole 'nother thing to put down.

I didn't understand the connection between my behaviors and addiction and neither did my sponsor. I had told her I was prostituting, and she told me to "get that money." I was honest with her but when I asked her about working the steps of the program, she said, "Oh baby, I don't work the steps." That's when I knew I had to get another sponsor.

I soon found a new sponsor, and around the same time, I got into a relationship with a man I had met in recovery. He had about seven years clean at the time. He eventually moved in with me. I was still tricking here and there but not telling anyone, not even my new sponsor. She and I were working on step one ("We admitted that we were powerless over our addiction, that our lives had become unmanageable"), but I wasn't being honest—not with myself or others. My new sponsor eventually told me that she was leaving the program. She was no longer my sponsor, and I was already lost. At that point I had not used yet, but I was tricking. .

My boyfriend was still living with me and all of the sudden he got custody of his son. I watched his son while he was at work. I also volunteered at the Rochester Fatherhood Resource Initiative. My boyfriend started selling cocaine. One morning in June 2004, he and his son were gone when I woke up. I thought, *I want to get high.* The drugs were easily accessible, right there in the apartment. I didn't have time to talk myself out of it. I walked to the corner store and bought a crack stem. You can buy crack stems at most corner stores in the 'hood. They are called "flowers" in the store. I went back to the apartment and filled the bathtub, lit some candles, got into the tub, and started smoking. My boyfriend came home and found me and said, "What do you want to do? Do you want to get some help?

Or do you want to smoke the package?"

I looked at him. He knew the answer. I had woken the monster up. The fat lady sang. It was curtains. He gave me the rest of it. He and his son soon moved out of my house because of what I was doing. He said he could not have his son around someone who was using drugs—but I guess daddy selling drugs was okay!

Once I started using, I lost my volunteer job at the Rochester Fatherhood Initiative. I wasn't showing up much, and when I did show up, I was getting high in the bathroom. I went to my outpatient group and told them that I used. There was one particularly important person I met in this group named Kim V. We had been influential in the group talking about the program and staying clean. When I relapsed, everyone's reaction was "Wow, you relapsed?!!" I told them, "Yeah, I'm an addict. It's not because the dog died or anything bad happened. I used because I wanted to use."

My counselor told me, "My concern for you is that your ego and pride are going to keep you out there, and you're not going to get the help that you need." I went to one more group meeting after that and then stopped because I continued to use. I lost my apartment in September 2004. DHS wasn't paying my rent because I stopped going to the group. I moved all my stuff to the houses of other addicts and they eventually sold all of it to buy drugs. I was homeless, going from place to place. I had hit yet another bottom and didn't have anywhere to go. I was sleeping with people to get out of the cold.

I sometimes stayed with a couple named Amiel and Janice. Amiel and I used to sit at the table, getting high, and talk about how we'd be clean someday. He's in recovery today, too, and I talk about that at meetings. I will say, "There's an addict in here who knows me, who used to get high with me, who's seen me at my worst. So, recovery is possible. We used to sit at the table getting high and talking about the day we were going to be clean. And now we're here, clean, the both of us. Who would have thought?"

For a while I stayed with a young man named Eric who I had

tricked with a few times. He lived on Emerson Street near Lake Avenue. He told me, "You can move in with me and do your tricks here." I knew he liked me but me turning tricks there turned out not to be an option. Apparently, he had feelings for me. He started telling my Johns that I was dead. I told him: "How do you expect me to pay rent if you're telling people that I'm dead? If you want me to pay rent and contribute and buy food, you have to stop doing that shit." I got tired of turning tricks in cars and on corners. I'd leave the house and turn tricks and sometimes be gone for days. Sometimes I'd turn a trick with Eric then go get some drugs and be gone. I had a cat named BamBam who lived with me. I loved BamBam. BamBam was my friend—the only one I could count on who didn't have any ulterior motives. Eric let BamBam go outside and I never saw that cat again.

While I was living with Eric, I got arrested on March 8, 2005 for prostitution. Prostitution is a misdemeanor in Rochester. I was sentenced to eight days in jail. When you're arrested for prostitution, you're tested for sexually transmitted diseases. But you don't get your results back while you're in jail.

After I got out, I was getting high one day at Eric's when two people showed up banging on the door like they were the police. Turns out they were from the Health Department.

"We're looking for Dellenna Harper."

I told them, "If you find the bitch, you tell the bitch, I want my money." I slammed the door in their faces.

I knew why they were there. I had gotten a letter from the Health Department stating I needed to come in for treatment as I had gonorrhea or chlamydia. I can't remember which. But I was too busy getting high to go down there and get a shot in the booty.

Eventually Eric got tired of my doings and put me out. All my clothes and everything were at his place and I was homeless again—staying with people or staying at drug houses and abandoned houses, doing what I had to do to survive.

I used to hang out at a house where some young dudes were

selling drugs. They didn't let people come in and smoke except for me. I have a way about me. One of them, Junior, used to tell me "You don't belong out here."

"Well, you don't either."

"Well, that makes two of us. Give me two bags for $20!"

Junior was not your typical drug dealer. He should have been in school somewhere. Unfortunately, he learned everything about the lifestyle the hard way, like I did. These dudes had large sums of money—like a thousand dollars or more—and their supplier, big guy, often came by to collect. I used to tell Junior, "You can't leave this kind of money laying around 'cuz if it comes up missing, I'm gonna be the first one they blame 'cuz I'm the crackhead."

One day the supplier and another guy came to collect their money, and Junior didn't have it. I told the big guy, "Look if I had the money, I'd been gone. I wouldn't be sittin' up here hanging around." They believed me because they knew that me, a crackhead, would be gone if I took that money.

They pushed me and Junior down to the basement. They made me watch while they beat him with two-by-fours and bats. They're taking turns hitting him and he can't stand 'cuz they broke one of his legs and they broke the other ankle. They put the dogs on him. They really did a number on him.

I sat there watching. I wasn't scared because down in Texas, I'd seen worse. Plus, I was high. I thought, *I told you not to leave that money. Why the fuck didn't you listen to me?* By this time, I was desensitized to the violence.

Finally, they brought us back upstairs, and they're still threatening us. They held us hostage for about five hours. Come to find out Junior's friend/partner who sells drugs there took the money as a joke. Either he called them, or they called him and he was like "Oh, I got the money." I thought, *Wow, do you realize they almost took Junior's life because of you and your shenanigans?*

The suppliers didn't let Junior go to the hospital for a few days because they knew hospital staff would ask questions.

After that happened, I stopped hanging out at that house. I did go back to check on Junior and buy drugs from him. He gave me money to go to the store to get what he needed and money to get something for me, too. His leg never did heal right.

Junior and I used to have really good conversations. I wasn't the kind of person who would get high and be trippin'. I could have a conversation while I was high. A lot of people have different tweaks when they're high. Some people like to grab knives. Some people can't talk. That wasn't me. I could hold a decent conversation while digging in my purse for God knows what. Digging in my purse for whatever was my tweak.

Several years after I got clean, I saw Junior working at a Chipotle cutting up the chicken, and I said, "You really look like a pro, like you know what you're doing."

He looked at me for a moment, and then he recognized me. "What's up?"

"Do you remember me?

"Yeah."

"I'm really glad to see you on this side."

"You look really good."

"You do too. You healed really good."

Going back to check on Junior at that house is another example of my little acts of kindness. It's like what that guy in Minnesota told me. "Dellenna, there is something about you and you don't belong here."

"Everybody's always saying that, but no one can tell me what it is that I have."

"I'm gonna tell you. You still have a heart and people out here don't have a heart. Out here it's do or die, survival of the fittest. Don't ever let this lifestyle or Satan take it from you. That's why you don't belong here."

Even in Rochester I was still feeding people, people that I didn't like, people who fought me yesterday. If you're hungry, I'm gonna feed you even knowing that you would stab me in the back again the next day.

This may sound funny, but I prayed for people who harmed me, asking God to give them everything I wanted for myself. I told God, "I don't mean a word of this shit, but I'm trying to do the right thing." I remember one time down in Texas this man raped me, and I prayed for him for a couple of nights because I knew that forgiving others for the harm that they have done to me was for me, not for them. For me to be forgiven for what I had done, I had to forgive others when they harmed me. I also believe that anybody in their right mind would not harm another human being; something had to have happened to the person to make them act like that towards others. That belief helped me to move towards forgiveness.

The man who raped me ended up apologizing. That meant everything to me—that apology. Yes, he violated me but the fact he came up to me, and he made a sincere apology meant so much. I thought, *Damn, this shit really works.* God knew; he knew my heart. I'm always praying for people that have harmed me.

I used to stay with this girl who people called Casper. She let me wear her clothes, and she styled my hair. She taught me how to be a better ho by reminding me that I had to keep myself up. She also taught me how to make more money by choosing which Johns to trick with. She always told me that white men pay more. They are more dangerous, but they pay more. She was right. She was an experienced prostitute. We were making money and getting high while I lived with her. When her kids sometimes visited, we had to put on this front that we were not getting high. She wasn't paying her bills. The water got shut off, the electricity got shut off, and the bathroom toilet was backed up, which produced this foul smell. One day, there was so much going on in the house—people selling, people using, people fighting, people tricking. I couldn't take it. I went in the bathroom with two or three other people and our Bibles, and we had a little Bible study. That was the only place in the house that wasn't smelling that day. I know that was God's doing because every other time that bathroom stunk. She ended up going to jail, and we had to vacate the apartment.

I moved in with this guy named Rodney. I stayed there awhile and paid rent for my room. It was a crack house. Rodney had a pit bull, but it wasn't a vicious dog. It acted like a puppy and ran away when it got scared. I loved that dog. One time when I was gone for a couple of days, a dealer beat up Rodney and broke the dog's leg.

This drug dealer moved other drug dealers into the house. Sometimes they gave me drugs and sometimes they didn't. Of course, I tricked with them; I tricked with whoever. One of the other dealers in the building told me, "You can't turn any dates in this building." He was mad because I wouldn't buy my drugs from him. I was like "whatever, you don't own the building." After that, I brought my dates in the back door.

Sometimes some of the women who prostituted came over and we got high and read the Bible. That may sound crazy but those are the times when I needed God the most. A lot of people might say, "You're going to hell for that." God knew I wanted to do the right thing but it's kinda hard when you're living in a crack house. You wake up and you say you're not gonna get high but at the first knock on the door, you're off to the races.

Those Bible studies are what brought some of us through and kept us sane. Not only would I get in His Word when things are going well, but I was in His Word when things were going bad. I was trying to keep my heart. I never wanted to lose my heart out there. I never did. I was praying for action because I thought about being clean. I wrote about it, I talked about it but never put any action behind it. I talked to my family at some point during that time and told my parents to pray for action for me.

One morning I brought a date in the front door and turned a trick in my bedroom. All of a sudden there was a banging on the bedroom door. I opened the door and it was the dealer who had told me I couldn't turn tricks in the building. I stepped in the hallway and closed the bedroom door behind me. He threatened me saying, "You got seventy-two hours to get out of Rochester, else I'm gonna kill you." I'm like "Bitch, please." When I came back into the bedroom, the window was open, and the curtains were blowing in the wind. My date got so scared that he climbed through the window. Fortunately, he had already paid me.

I left the house and walked down the street. I'm thinking, *This is the morning from hell.* I'm praying, *God, just help me with action, please help me with action. I'm tired of this shit. I'm tired of living like this. I'm so tired.* I wanted to stop using many times but couldn't because I was caught up in the grips of the drugs and the lifestyle.

I walked down Montrose Street to North Plymouth Avenue, and before I got to the end of the block, two guys pulled up in a car. I got in, and we negotiated a transaction. And then they told me they were the police.

"Thank God," I said.

They looked at me like *what?*

"Man, you just don't know." I felt so relieved.

It was Feb. 16, 2006. God had answered my prayers.

7

From jail to the Jennifer House

When the undercover cops arrested me, they handcuffed me and drove me to a parking lot behind a big building at Dewey Avenue and Driving Park. They put me in a paddy wagon with the other prostitutes they'd picked up in a sting. Then they went back out and arrested more prostitutes. I remember that day vividly. I sat in the paddy wagon desperately wanting to go to jail. After they'd arrested about thirty prostitutes, they drove us to the jail and booked us. All the prostitutes were crowded into a small room. It had a little toilet in a half cubicle that came up to my waist. When I was sitting on this cold metal toilet, the guards could see me from the shoulders up.

I knew if I got a couple clean days under my belt, I could do the right thing. But I couldn't get an hour clean. The crack had a hold on me, and I was caught up in its grip. The movie *New Jack City* is one of the most realistic movies about the lifestyle. Chris Rock plays a character called Pookie. He's got this girlfriend and they're both crackheads. He says, "You used to be a prom queen, now you're a crack fiend." I was never a prom queen, but I relate because I was popular in high school. In the movie, Pookie gets clean and goes undercover for the cops to help them catch a drug dealer. But Pookie relapses, and he says, "It's calling me," meaning the drugs are calling him. It's true. I felt immensely relieved that I had been arrested. I had always told myself I would be clean one day; I had to survive the jungle. I had to live to see that day.

But that relief didn't last long, and a battle started raging inside me. The other prostitutes started coming up with a plan that when they got released from jail, they were going get high, and I was going along with them. *But wait; a minute ago I felt relieved, and I wanted to stay clean.* Part of me wanted to go back to what I was familiar with—the drugs, the misery, and the pain. I knew what to expect. The other part of me wanted to do something different, but I was terrified because I didn't know what to expect.

After spending a day or two at the downtown jail, we were transported to the jail facility in the suburb of Henrietta. Normally, when you are jailed for prostitution, you stay at the jail downtown for seven or eight days before you get out. The Henrietta jail was for people staying longer. There was one big room with about twenty-five sets of bunk beds and a common area where we could watch TV and sit down and eat. Henrietta was a lot better than the downtown jail. In Henrietta, there were windows and a gym where the air felt fresh and we could see the sky through the ceiling. At the jail downtown, there were no windows—stale air, roaches, and jail cells; it was depressing.

One morning at the Henrietta jail, another prostitute (I called her "Little Bobblehead" because of the way she bobbed her head up and down) came to my cubicle and said, "Come on, "Baby Dee", let's go to this group."

I didn't want to go. "Get the fuck out of my cubicle." All I wanted was to sleep.

But something inside me said, *Just get up and go to this group.* I believe it was my spirit talking. About ten of us sat in a circle and introduced ourselves. A woman named Judy and another woman named Renee were leading the group. They talked about a place called the Jennifer House. I wanted to do something different, but I didn't have anywhere to go—not anywhere safe. I didn't have income. I didn't have anything. I didn't have a plan. Judy said you're more than welcome to come to the house when you get out of jail if you want to; however, if you don't want to come to the house, we would still love to have you in the group. Judy asked me a question—I don't remember what—and I answered, "I tell people what they want to hear. I want some help but I'm always telling people what they want to hear to get my needs met."

To get admitted to the Jennifer House, you had to sign a contract. Judy had one contract left, and she had handed it to Little Bobblehead. But she was on the fence about whether she wanted to go there. I said, "I'll go" because I'm thinking, *This is my chance; this is the answer to my prayers.* Judy politely snatched the contract out of Little Bobblehead's hand and gave it to me. I've never seen someone politely snatch something out of someone's hand like that.

Later, Judy told me she gave me that contract because "you told me you tell people what they want to hear. You told on yourself."

I signed the contract. That was on a Wednesday. I was getting out of jail on Friday. I told the jail guard, "Please make sure that that woman from the Jennifer House is here to pick me up because if she's not, I'm going with these other women to get high."

"Well, don't go," the guard told me.

"You don't understand. I don't want to die. Please make sure that lady is here."

When Friday came, I was feeling really anxious. I wanted to go use but a part of me was like *No, try this. You're done.* When we were released, I was planning to go outside and smoke a cigarette, but before I got out the door, I heard a woman loudly calling "Deleeennnna Haarrrperrr!" Although I felt relieved when I heard that loud voice and the way the woman said my name, I wondered what the hell did I get myself into.

Wanda from the Jennifer House was there to pick me up and just in time. If she had not been there that day, I would have gone with the other prostitutes to get high.

When I speak to groups about my arrival at the Jennifer House, I tell them, "I basically slid under the door." It was such a low point in my life. I was fearful and consumed with shame and guilt. I was broken both mentally and spiritually. I was tired, tired of who I had become and tired of the way that I had been living. I had this gift called desperation. I was so beaten by the streets and the drugs. This state of desperation birthed in me the willingness and open-mindedness to do whatever I needed to do. All I knew was my way was not working. That gift of desperation helped me to accept help from others to guide and direct me, which led me to stop digging a deeper bottom.

When I slid under the door of the Jennifer House, I felt this overwhelming sense of peace. My heart quietly spoke to me and said, "We're home." The other residents were very welcoming, and when I saw all the food in the pantry—oh my God—the angels started singing. That became my favorite place in the house, and it was right next to the refrigerator.

The Jennifer House is a unique home in a Rochester neighborhood. The Jennifer House is for women who are coming out of prison, jail, inpatient treatment, the streets, or other homeless situations and who struggle with substance abuse and mental health issues. The Jennifer House is part of the Spiritus Christi Prison Outreach, which is a ministry of Spiritus Christi Church in Rochester.

At the Jennifer House, I had two roommates. Because I had been in halfway houses before, I knew how to live with structure. But in the other houses, I'd always gotten high. This time I was so desperate. I pretty much did what they told me to do—at least at first. I was finally learning to apply the information I had picked up at all the treatment centers along the way and put that information on a shelf in my head.

In the drug lifestyle, I never really trusted anyone because I was not trustworthy. I burned you the first chance I got, to get my drugs. At the Jennifer House, I started learning that those previous "principles" were not conducive to my recovery. I had to change. People believed in me before I believed in myself. People trusted me before I trusted myself. I trusted others before I trusted myself.

Early on, one of the staff at the Jennifer House Samone sent me to the store to get her some cigarettes. She gave me twenty dollars. I looked at her thinking, *You trust me with this? Don't you know who I am and where I come from, what I did?* I was literally shocked. She did not bat an eye when she gave me that money. Because of that I was determined to do the right thing.

I walked to the store and I bought the cigarettes. I made sure to get the receipt. I walked back to the Jennifer House, and when I got there, I was in tears. Samone was the first person who trusted in me. "What's wrong, nobody's trusted you?" she asked. I said no, and she hugged me.

In the past, people didn't give me their money. No one did that because they knew me. My famous words were "I'll be right back," and I never came back. Or maybe I'd come back a month or two later, like I did in Texas.

At the Jennifer House, I got connected to a mental health therapist and an outpatient program. I started going to twelve-step meetings. I needed to get a sponsor. At one meeting, I saw this woman in a pantsuit wearing a really sharp hat. She was the only white lady there. I recognized her from when I was in recovery when I first came to Rochester before I relapsed. We had been in a group together. I asked her to be my sponsor. Kim helped me deal with the things going on at the house and in group. What she really did, though, was she helped me deal with me.

Kim and I later understood that God put us together that first time in group. We didn't realize then that He was setting us up to be together later.

My time at the Jennifer House was a lot different than at the other halfway houses where I'd lived. The other times I came into recovery and accumulated a lot of clothes and other stuff really fast, thinking I was recovering. This time I was patient. I did without. Because I didn't ask my mom and dad for money, I was still tricking here and there to get money for cigarettes. I smoked lot of cigarettes. But tricking didn't feel right, so I stopped. The tricking I did while at the Jennifer House did not involve sex. That is how I justified it in my mind. I was getting money from men by manipulation. I knew they liked me and used that to my advantage. That, in my eyes, is still prostitution.

The Jennifer House staff connected me to a chemical dependency outpatient program at Huther Doyle on East Avenue in Rochester. I participated in a group there three times a week. I started out in what's called "phase one" for people early in their recovery.

After every group session, some of the others fired up a blunt after we walked out of the building and headed to the bus stop. I had to catch a certain bus because I had a curfew, so I couldn't take a detour to catch a different bus. I walked ahead of them. I tried walking behind them, but the wind blew the smell of weed back in my face.

I felt angry because they were getting high. It wasn't that I couldn't get high, I chose not to. Every day in group, we had to say if we had used drugs. Some of them were honest, and some weren't. Some of the people using drugs were being moved into "phase two" before people further along in their recovery. I wasn't moved up, and I got angry about it. *Here I am staying clean and these others are moving to the next phase.* This outpatient program used "the harm reduction model", which is based on the idea that if you're not smoking crack as much as you used to, or you're no longer smoking crack but smoking weed—which is considered less harmful—then you're successful.

I have to abstain completely from drugs because the other stuff will bring me back to my drug of choice. That has been my experience. In the past, I had tried the marijuana program where I smoked only weed and not crack. That did not work for me. I tried sticking to alcohol but that did not work for me either. Sooner or later I always ended up with what I really wanted and that was crack. I talked to Kim about my anger about not moving into phase two.

I told her I was going to twelve-step meetings, I had a sponsor, I was doing everything I needed to do. "Well, Dellenna, maybe you're there for a reason. Keep showing up," she told me.

That's what I did. I decided not to push it. I surrendered and accepted it. Eventually I moved up to phase two.

When I was released from jail, I was put on probation for ninety days. I had to check in with my probation officer once a week and go to Judge Rainbow Morse's court once a month, as did the other thirty or so women that I was arrested with. Every time I went to court, fewer women showed up. Finally, the last time, only two of us showed up. We were the only ones who made it ninety days. I later found out that the other woman fell off.

At the Jennifer House, we each had to fill out a weekly schedule. It was posted in the office and the staff had to approve the schedule. We could not just go where we wanted to go when we wanted to go. We had to follow our schedules.

I often got in trouble for being somewhere that I wasn't supposed to be. I might have "library" on my schedule, but I'd be somewhere hanging out. The staff always saw me, and they made sure I knew they'd seen me, calling out to me, "Hey, Dellenna, hi, see you back at the house." I'd act all nonchalant.

Never once did it cross my mind that I'm not going back to the house. I always went back to the house and took the consequences. I usually followed my schedule to go to the twelve-step meetings and any important appointments like group or the doctor, but I was doing other things too, like hooking up with guys.

The main reason I deviated from my schedule a lot was men. I had all kinds of boyfriends. I'd come back to the Jennifer House with roses, and Judy would ask, "Where you'd get the roses from?"

"I bought 'em."

I was very quick to lie. The Jennifer House had a rule that you couldn't be in a relationship. But how realistic is that? When a person goes into recovery, the first thing most people do is get into a relationship. I met guys in the twelve-step meetings. It wasn't like we were doing anything; we were hanging out in the park or going to the library. Anything to do with a man, I had to sneak to do it, because I wasn't supposed to be in a relationship. It would have been much easier if I could have said, "I'm going to the park with so-and-so."

"Who's so-and-so?"

"A guy I met in the program."

I still struggled with desiring attention from men. By now I know they were a distraction to me. I had a void that the drugs left, and I was trying to fill the void with flesh. I was not using drugs anymore, but I was using men. My disease was manifesting itself in the form of needing the attention of men.

I began learning the importance of sticking to my schedule. I knew that if I felt like using, as long as I stuck to my schedule, I'd be successful that day. I was soon able to recognize that when I deviated from my schedule, as I did sometimes, it was not healthy, nor was it conducive to my recovery as I was being sneaky and deceitful not only to staff but also to myself. I was working really hard at being honest.

I liked walking to the public library that was close by. I checked my email there because that was my only contact with my mom and dad. I could only make two long-distance calls a week. I was determined to rebuild the relationship with my family. I was trying to take it slow. Instead of telling them how I was doing, I wanted to show them. I knew that was going to take time. I had let them down many, many times in the past—going in and out of programs and getting their hopes up only to disappoint them, again and again. I knew this time would be different. I had to take it slow and easy to regain their trust.

I also liked going to the library because I like to read. One book I found during that time is *Coldest Winter Ever* by Sister Souljah. Winter is the name of this really bad ass chick who is incredibly street savvy. Some people thought the books I was reading weren't healthy for me. I weened myself off my former lifestyle by reading about it. I was addicted to the lifestyle not only the drugs. The lifestyle was harder for me to give up than the drugs were.

While I was living at the Jennifer House, I had to face the reality of my behavior in the weekly one-on-one meetings with my case manager, Wanda—the same woman who picked me up at the jail. She constantly called me on my behavior.

"What are you talking about?" I'd say. At the time, I thought it was stupid. But what she said was valid. I couldn't see it then.

I learned in the twelve-step program that I shouldn't keep secrets. When I broke the Jennifer House rules, I told my sponsor Kim. She'd say, "Dellenna, you're not telling the person that's going to hold you accountable."

"Exactly. That's why I'm telling you. I didn't want to keep the secret. I don't care about being held accountable."

"You have to tell the people who are going to hold you accountable."

She meant that I had to tell on myself, which was why Judy had given me that application for the Jennifer House.

Wanda and I butted heads a lot. I told her, "I know you don't like me, and I don't like you, but you have a job to do and that's to help me because I don't want to die."

Wanda didn't say it, but she looked at me and her eyes said *Shut up*.

I'd say, "As long as we're on the same page, I'll shut up now."

Eventually, she'd lose patience and put me out of her office. "Get out."

I laugh about it now.

One time, Wanda changed my schedule to attend a baptism of another resident. Wanda had crossed off what I had on the schedule and written "Baptism with so-and-so."

I told her, "I want to go and support her. How dare you change my schedule?! That's not right. You need to ask me. Give me a choice."

I called her on that stuff. I'm good at debate. "In all the treatment centers, all the halfway houses, all the detox centers, all the programs, I've picked up information so I know what I need to do, and this shit you're telling me makes absolutely no sense. And you're sitting there trying to make it make sense to me."

The way Wanda talked to me was what I needed—that brutal honesty, that roughness, that rawness. Don't sugar coat nothing with me because when I was using, the tricks, the drugs, and the disease of addiction didn't sugar coat anything. That was a real rough, raw life. When I came into recovery, I needed that. I'm grateful she was that person. Wanda called it out like it is, brutally honest. And Kim was like that, too.

At the Jennifer House, the staff taught us and loved us until we were able to love ourselves.

At the same time, I worked closely with my sponsor, Kim. She gave me an assignment from the twelve-step program. Every day, I wrote down answers to questions that were in a pamphlet, making a daily inventory of *Living the Program.*

This is one of my first entries, dated March 13, 2006.

"Am I clean today?" *Yes.*

How did I act differently? *I did a lot of things today for other people for the right reasons.*

My disease did not run my life today. God did.

I don't regret doing anything today. I walked in the spirit today.

I wish I would have been able to spend more time in Bible today.

I was good to myself today.

I did not use and accomplished/followed thru w/everything on schedule.

Today was a Blessed day.

I had a happy, joyous day.

Yes, my day was serene.

Most days I wrote in this journal, answering the questions, usually filling up a couple pages. I started each entry noting "I am clean." I also told on myself in this journal. On March 15, I wrote:

I am clean today. I am actually following thru on things I set out to do. My disease did not run my life today but I had moments with it today. After going to the library, I had sex and had feelings behind it. I had planned on practicing abstinence. I wish I would not have hooked up with him cuz in the JH I'm not supposed to do men cuz I need to do me. So I lost focus cuz I did him and liked it. I wish I had not gone behind people's back to hook up with. I don't like to lie. I was good to myself today. I stayed clean. Today was a good day. I was happy. Just went thru feelings behind choices today. I was serene… I am powerless today. I trust my HP. I learned I am able to make mistakes and forgive myself… I obsessed about letting God down for violating my temple, I asked for forgiveness. God gave me another day and another day clean….By breaking rules I could have harmed myself. By keeping this secret, I jeopardize my recovery, which if jeopardized will lead to harming others as well. I am willing to change today.

I did pray and meditate today. That's when I asked for forgiveness and forgave myself. I am grateful for love and forgiveness. staying clean and my relationship with God.

March 28, 2006

I am clean today. I acted as if I was a part of something today. I also acted differently by eating a piece of humble pie. My disease has been all in the midst. I HAVE NO Business talking to A MAN CUZ I Get attached and defocused and I need to get to know myself and I get distracted easy. I don't need a man to validate me. For some reason I think I do…I am powerless over the situation I am in but not how I react to the situation. I learned my disease is smarter than I thought. I learned humility. Real Good…I did admit fault today…I was asking myself was it really that bad. I came to the conclusion that it wasn't yet, but it would have been so they are just helping me nip in bud right now…I need to move the men out of the way so I can work on me.

On April 1, 2006, I wrote:

I wish I had not gone to Burger King. I could've called and asked. But I didn't. And when I returned, I still didn't say anything.

But two days later, I wrote I acted differently today by being responsible. Today was a long day. I followed my schedule to a T … I learned today that even if I get tired and bored of my daily routine I cannot stop. It's OK for me to try new healthy activities but I have to stick to the basics, mainly my praying and journaling. I must stay connected.

I also realized that I had to deal with the consequences when I deviated from my schedule, if I got caught. And I got caught a lot.

On April 12, I revealed in my journal:

I acted differently by not following my schedule. My disease was in my life today. I was deceitful. Going to a meeting was on my schedule and I did not go. I wish I would have followed my schedule.

The next day, I noted:

I acted differently by not deviating from my schedule…I did not attend a meeting today cuz I am on punishment for deviating from my schedule…I am powerless over other people's choices. There seems to be a whole lot of women doing a whole lot of shit and getting away with it. I'm powerless over this. I trusted God today. I learned I need to focus on me. No matter what happens, I need to focus on me…I accept and love myself today.

My resolve didn't last long. The next day, April 14, I wrote:

I acted differently by still deviating from my schedule. For some reason, I think the rules don't apply to me. The disease did not run my life but by me deviating from schedule it was in the midst. I don't regret going to library and checking email. I just hated the feeling of watching my back…I am powerless of my punishment. It is the consequences of my behavior. I trust God today. I learned that for some reason I seem to think the rules don't apply to me. I need to work on that.

In the twelve-step program, we're taught that staying clean must come first. Staying clean was always on my mind. I knew as long as I did not pick up the drugs, I had a chance to stop practicing unhealthy behaviors.

April 8, I wrote: *I acted differently by not entertaining a thought I had. I was in a meeting. Had a thought. I played the entire scenario out in my head from beginning to end. I concluded that it was not a good idea, said a prayer, sat and listened, and I was ok. My disease did not run my life but it did pop up*

clump of hair out. She and I looked at each other in shock. There was a long moment of silence. I did not know what to say; I felt bad for her. I could not imagine how she felt at that moment. A day or two later, there was a knock on my apartment door. When I opened the door, I saw this beautiful, tall, and completely bald woman standing in my doorway. Simone was even more beautiful without hair. "You're gorgeous," I told her. She took her power back by shaving her head. Not everyone can rock that look. But she did. Sometimes she went to twelve-step meetings with nothing covering her head, and other times she wore a wig. She had these different looks going on depending on how she felt that day.

One thing Simone taught me was to keep my recovery first. Before her diagnosis, we always walked or caught the bus to twelve-step meetings. But after she started chemotherapy, she was getting weaker and weaker. At times, we still walked to meetings. And it might take us a little longer to get there, but we still went. Her recovery remained as important to her as mine did to me.

Simone inspired me because she did not let the cancer stop her. She continued to do regular activities as much as she could. It took her twenty minutes to get downstairs at the YWCA using her walker; it used to take less than five. She'd say, "Let's go smoke a cigarette." I wouldn't say anything to her about smoking, like "You know you got cancer; you shouldn't be smoking." She didn't want to hear it. Then we would come back upstairs. Twenty minutes later, "Let's go smoke a cigarette," she'd say. "Damn, Simone, we just smoked." But I got back up, and we walked back downstairs and smoked another cigarette.

As time went on, Simone got sicker and sicker. I took turns with the ladies that had moved from the Jennifer House being with Simone. I came into recovery with traits of self-obsession and self-centeredness, and those traits made me want to keep walking past Simone's room when she was sick. I didn't want to see her like that, but I told myself, *It's not about me. She needs me now.* I always acknowledged the fact that I didn't want to go in there but was able to recognize that I needed to and did it anyway. Jeannette, my counselor at the YWCA, taught me to acknowledge that. She was the bomb counselor at the YWCA. Everybody hated her; they couldn't stand her because she was brutally honest. But she said what she had to say with love and compassion. I never could deny the truth of what she said.

Jeanette talked to me about Simone and helped me to find balance with taking care of Simone and taking care of me, too, because I had to take care of me. One week I didn't go to my twelve-step meetings because I was with Simone. I had many feelings and didn't know how to express them. I felt fearful and sad for my friend. I missed my family and felt regret because my dad had cancer and I was not there for him. I felt guilty and ashamed of the things I had done and the people I had hurt. I felt shameful for not being a mother to my child. I was all over the place with my feelings.

Jeanette helped me to get back on track. We would talk about all this stuff that happened to me, and then she'd say, "Our time is up." But I wasn't ready to stop; I was just getting started. She opened up the Pandora's box of my feelings and emotions. I did not know how to close it up and move on with my day. I learned to schedule my meeting with Jeannette in the morning and then go to a twelve-step meeting afterward. The meeting gave me a safe place to process my feelings. Soon after, Jeanette taught me how to compartmentalize. I learned to put my feelings in a box, so to speak, and place the box on the shelf. Then we could come back to them in our next session or I could process them with my mental health therapist or process them with paper and pen in my journal.

Knowing how to compartmentalize my feelings isn't always healthy for me. I have to consciously remember to go back into my little cupboard and feel these feelings otherwise my feelings can overtake me—the guilt, shame, sadness, regret, and anger. If I do not process those feelings, I start making decisions based on my emotions, and that's not a good place to be in recovery.

One time I went to visit Simone in the hospital, and she was out of it. She had the TV on but no volume, and I said, "What you doin' with the TV on and no volume? Turn the volume up, Simone." She felt around on the bed and hit the button, but it was not the remote for the TV. It was the morphine. She got a dose of morphine and her eyes rolled back in her head. She was high as hell. I laugh about that today, but I do realize she was in a lot of pain at times.

A friend of ours, Sam, brought her a fake plastic bird in a wooden cage. The bird chirped when it was turned on. He thought the bird might cheer Simone. That damn bird chirped during his entire visit. I liked it at first but then it got annoying. "Chiiiirrrp, chirp, chirp, chirp, chirp, chiiiirrrrp, chirp, chirp, chirp, chirp." It was a nice visit, but after he left, Simone said, "Dellenna, get that god damn bird outta my room." I brought the bird home with me. I have it to this day, but I don't have batteries in it.

Simone was in and out of the hospital. She was stubborn and would leave the hospital without being discharged. Deep down in my heart I knew that one time she was going to be admitted to the hospital and not return to the YWCA, but my mind was still in denial. It was a long time before I surrendered to the fact that Simone was dying.

As she got worse, a grieving group got together at the YWCA for all the women who wanted to talk. This feisty nurse named Mary Ellen led those stupid groups, and I'm being sarcastic by calling them stupid. I would say, "You guys are writing her off like she's already fucking dead. She's right upstairs; she's not dead; she's not gonna die. You guys are stupid for having this group." I was the last one to accept that Simone was going to die because I'd tell her, "I got faith in God and hope for you. I'm hoping and believing for you. You can give up, but I believe for you. God didn't bring you into this process of recovery only to have you die a year later."

I think Mary Ellen was a nun. I loved her. Sometimes she came to the State of the Heart meetings at the Jennifer House. Mary Ellen made the most beautiful birthday cakes for the women. What's crazy is that Mary Ellen, who prepared us for Simone's death, died three days before Simone did. She died of an asthma attack alone in her apartment. I believe that when Simone died, Mary Ellen was at the Pearly Gates to welcome her.

By the time Simone passed, I had accepted she was going to die. Everyone was like trippin' when they heard. In the black culture when people die, some people grieve in a dramatic way like wailing and falling on the floor. I called people to let them know and some of them flipped out. I wondered, *Why am I not responding like that?* I think it was because I had my closure with her.

I said everything that I needed to say to her while she was still alive; she said everything that she needed to say to me. I was at peace with her going. That's why I didn't respond like others did. I spent the most time with her of anyone. Everyone took turns being with her, but I spent the night with her. We had these conversations—conversations about death and all kinds of stuff that everybody's scared to talk about. It was helpful to me, and I like to believe it was helpful to her. She was my friend who taught me how to be a friend, how to show up for people. She taught me the meaning of love and selflessness because I did a lot of things for her that I didn't know I could do. She knew I loved her, and I knew she loved me. It's a blessing to be a part of someone's last days on this earth but I didn't realize it at the time. Her courage was amazing.

Simone taught me that my recovery must come first, no matter what. She introduced me to all these women who were a part of her life. They were living at Liberty Manor, a residential program for women in recovery. I inherited her support network, and they are my friends to this day. God brings people into your life, and you don't know whether it's for a moment or a season. I embraced the moment that Simone was in my life and learned so much from her. Without Simone's support network, I don't know where I would be. They are some phenomenal women; I call them my dream team. They're as crazy as I am. Some of them didn't like me at first because of my light skin and long hair, but once they got to know me, they were like "you're all right."

I'm forever grateful to Simone. She died a couple days before her one-year anniversary of being clean. In recovery we celebrate with yearly coins. Infinity coins are for those that die clean. Her home group gave her infinity coin to me. I had never experienced anything like what I went through with Simone. It was an awesome part of my journey. It was very tough, but it was a growth process. I had a spiritual awakening where I was able to practice a whole lot of spiritual principles. Being able to apply the principles took me away from my self-centeredness and self-obsession, which is the core of the disease of addiction. I learned early on in my journey of recovery that the people I start this process with may not be the people I continue it with. People will come into my life and then leave, while some will stay. Many will relapse, some will move away, while others die. I learned to get connected to people in my life, and when they are gone, cherish the moment in time I had with them. I cherish my time with the ones that stay as well.

When I lived at the YWCA, I was very protective of my recovery. I always told the other residents, "If I see any of you doing something that you have no business doing, and you're jeopardizing my recovery, I'm telling. I will tell on you because I take my recovery seriously, and this is my safe haven. If you're bringing shit up in here and you jeopardize my recovery, I will tell on your ass, and I hope you do the same thing for me."

One time a woman came back to the YWCA high as hell. I could tell she had been smoking crack as she had the crackjaw with her mouth moving from left to right, back and forth, over and over. I said, "Come on, let's go." I took her to one of the counselor's office, who was on the phone at the time. I knocked and said, "She needs to talk to you about something." I pushed her in the office and shut the door.

I never forgot what it was like for me when I moved into the YWCA with no TV or radio, no phone—just silence and four walls. I bought TVs real cheap and gave them away to the new women coming into the YWCA to live. There's a little gated park on the corner of North Clinton Avenue and Bittner Street, and a lot of people came there at night selling things. I bought several TVs from people who were on drugs. They'd ask for $30 or $50 and I'd talk them down to $10 or $15. I would think, I can't pass that up, a TV for $10! When the women, mainly from the Jennifer House, moved into the YWCA, I had a TV for them.

Eventually I got a job at the Healthy Sisters Soup and Bean Works in the basement of Catholic Family Center at 55 Troup Street. Healthy Sisters was a job-readiness program for women in recovery. We packaged dried soup mixes, jellybeans, and dips for sale. Simone connected me to her friend, Michelle, who was the supervisor. The program taught us about simple stuff that a lot of people just take for granted such as learning time management so you show up for work on time and call in to tell your supervisor if you aren't coming to work. I'd had jobs before, so I knew the basics of keeping a job. I take direction very well, and I'm all about efficiency. I worked my way up to a position called Quality Control.

Connie, another friend of Simone's, was another supervisor. Connie helped me a lot by showing me the ropes. She was a great teacher and leader. We went to festivals to sell the products. Each product had the woman's name who packed it written on the label. We'd call out "Healthy Sisters Soup and Bean Works! We got soup. Soup for sale! It's a good day for some soup. We got the magic jelly-beans. They are good stocking stuffers."

"What makes them magic?"

"If you eat one, the other jellybeans mysteriously disappear."

The customers loved that; they ate that up. We had a lot of fun at the festivals. I was trustworthy; the supervisor knew if Connie and I were there, nothing came up missing, which sometimes happened with other people. Although the project was for women in recovery, not everyone was practicing recovery. The program really helped me.

I learned a lot living at the YWCA. Although Jeannette was my assigned counselor, I utilized all the counselors—all of them. The director of the program, Amy, had an office right next to my apartment. When I woke up in the morning, I knocked on the wall and she knocked back. When I had about eighteen months clean, a counselor named Viola met with me and said, "Dellenna, I remember when you first got here, and you were going to court in stilettos and your little short skirts and your tank tops and lookin'..." Here she paused.

"Like a little whore?"

"Well, I wasn't going to say that."

"Well, I'll say it for you."

"And look at you now."

I don't think I was dressed for court that day, but I was dressed up to go somewhere. I was changing; I was growing. I was being more mindful of the clothes that I wore and other things, too. Viola noticed that. The staff watched me grow up at the YWCA.

After I moved to the YWCA, I got my own phone. I was able to call my family more. I missed Jallanna with all my heart. I was struggling with the fact that I was not physically raising my daughter. I really did not know who she was. I didn't know what her favorite color was, what she liked to eat, or who her best friend was. Someone suggested I get a notebook and write to her daily. So, I bought a journal and put Jallanna's photo on the cover. On the inside I wrote,

This book is for Jallanna. It's letters letting you know how much I miss you, love you and think about you. I just want this to be one of the many ways we get to know each other. I focus a lot on my feelings because they are important to get in touch with. I hope you enjoy.

I planned to give this journal to Jallanna when she turned 16, but I still write in it now and then, and she is in her 20s.

The first entry is dated Friday, June 16, 2006, 9:07 p.m.

Hello, Jallanna. I bought this notebook for you today. Since I moved here to the YWCA, I have more time on my hands. I wanted to let you know how much I love you and there is not one day that goes by that I don't think about you. After talking to you the other day, I realize that I really don't know you. That didn't make me feel good.

I have not been in your life like I should have been. I am sorry for that. I

wish I could turn back time but I can't change the past. Out of everything that has happened and all of the time that has went by, I need you to know one thing. I love you more than life itself. When I did drugs, I did things that hurt a lot of people. I didn't mean to. But I hurt you, my mom, Dad, Paul, Rita, Walter, Peggy, April, Sharon, Aunt Gloria, Rhonda, Uncle Don, Roxanne. Bottom line I hurt everyone that loved me. I hurt myself as well. Drugs made me do things a person would normally not do.

I can't express how much I love you. I know my actions said otherwise. But my heart says I love you. I am sorry for not being there for you. I don't know what to say. There is nothing I can say right now. I feel shameful, remorseful, and guilty for not being there for you. But right now, you are in the best place on earth w/Grandma and Grandpa. You see they stepped up to take care of you when I couldn't because of the drugs. I will have four months clean tomorrow off drugs. I'm just now learning to take care of myself. One day in the future in God's time not ours we will be together. I have to stay clean. And it will take time. I wish I could hold you right now. I have much to tell you on one hand and now on the other hand, I don't know what to say. I am going to take my time. I love you. Did I tell you I love you? Oh, yeah, I love you.

I tried to get to know Jallanna through phone calls. I knew I wasn't ready for her to visit me in Rochester and I also understood that my family was not going to let her come and see me yet. I was afraid to go back to St. Paul because I didn't want to relapse. Here are some entries from the journal.

June 23, 2006, 11:01 p.m.
Shoe 3 ½ kids
5-6 women's
Favorite color sky blue or light green
Best friend Ashly, Jordan, Brittney, Jesse and Logan
Boyfriend Tony or Terry Scott
Oh my GOD, my baby has a boyfriend.

Jallanna, I just got off the phone w/u. I was crying telling you I love you and I'm sorry for not being there. I told you some other things too. I also expressed how I want to get to know you and have a relationship w/you. I am trying and I'm not gonna give up. I told you a long time ago not to give up on me and I am not gonna give up on me or me and you having a relationship. I love you, Jallanna, BIG MUCH INFINITY 2006. I hope to talk to you tomorrow. (Big much infinity means I love you much forever.)

July 8, 2006 11:16 p.m.

Hey Baby, I hope you had a nice time at Rita's. You went to Eric's B-day. I went to MusicFest. I saw Avant, Baby Sham, Sincere, and I had to leave so I missed Busta Rhymes. I have a curfew so I had to be home at 7 p.m. I got me and you a leather anklet with shells on it. I hope you like it. I had a good day. The weather was nice. Even though I'm happy right now, a part of me is sad. Some of my friends relapsed and are back using drugs, and that scares me. I don't want to go back to that. I have lost too much time of my life and yours because of drugs. I don't want to go back. I'm scared for them. I can't do anything but pray for them. I have to take care of me, I don't go back out. Overall today was a good day. Most of all I got to talk to you. I miss u and love you. Big much infinity 2006 4ever and a day. Good night Sweetie.

P.S. The moon is beautiful tonight.

July 10, 2006 10:59 p.m.

Hey girl, how R U? I hope you had fun swimming today. I had a good day. Went to a 12-step meeting then to group, then I went to a friend's house and watched Pirates of the Caribbean. I didn't get to see the whole thing 'cuz I have a 7 p.m. curfew. Looks like a good movie. I wanted to let you know I was thinking of you. I wanted to tell you I love you. 4 ever and a day. Big Much Infinity 2006.

P.S. Another one of my neighbors didn't come back. I'm scared for her. I think she relapsed. Usually when people don't come back that usually means they went back out. The disease of addiction ain't nothing to play with. After the first drink or drug when somebody goes back out after being clean and sober, it's hard to stop and stay stopped. It's hard to come back and face the consequences and the people you love who are the people you hurt.

I know how they felt because I've been there. I know their pain because I've felt it. The hardest thing to do after a relapse is come back. Just like after telling a lie, it's hard to come back and admit that you lied. It's hard to admit when you're wrong. It's hard for people to admit when they messed up. I know now it's ok to be wrong and I make mistakes 'cuz I'm human.

I know today that I don't have to use no matter what. Please keep praying for me. Because sometimes I want to use. But I choose not to. As long as I don't use, I have a choice. If I use, I lose everything. So just for today I didn't use. Good night.

July 20, 2006 9:36 p.m.

Hey, Llannas, I hope you had a nice day today. My dad is in intensive care as you already know. I wish I could be there. I am powerless over the whole situation, and that doesn't feel too good. I miss all of you. Thank you for being there w/Grandpa. I know he can be hard to get along with at times but he loves you so much. Be easy on him.

He is funny 'cuz he fusses so much. I know he fusses at you a lot. He used to fuss at me, too. I miss him fussing at me. Yeah, I do. But He loves us. He fusses at people he loves. Well, baby girl, I just wanted to say hello and good night. I love you 4ever and a day. Big much infinity 2006. Good night Silly.

July 31, 2006 9:50 p.m.

Hey Baby Girl, I've been thinking about you today. I miss you. I wanted to tell you that. I went to a meeting the other day and people were talking about the problems they r having with their kids and I got angry and jealous 'cuz you're not with me. Angry at me because it's my fault you are not with me and jealous because you are not with me. It also encouraged me because I know that if I keep doing what I'm doing, God's will, you will be with me one day. I think about that day a lot. I am anxious to get you in my life and scared also because I don't know how to be a mom to you. But we will learn when that time comes. I love you BIG MUCH and I wanted you to know that. Good night.

Oct. 1, 2006 11:05 p.m.

Hey baby, you got a cell phone. You called me and left me some messages today. That made my week. It felt soooo good to come home and get a message from you. I saved it. I was happy. I called you back and you were at a spaghetti dinner for hockey or something. I hope you had fun. You told me your favorite subjects in school are history and English and your favorite teacher is Mrs. Simmer who teaches cooking and sewing. You are growing up fast. I can't believe you are in the 7th grade already. I hate I missed you growing up because of those stupid drugs. I hate drugs. Well, I just wanted to write you real quick. I love you forever and a day. Good night, Sweetie. I love you big much.

Oct. 11, 2006 4:10 p.m.

I'm crying for you right now because Grandma called me and we talked. I miss you, my mom and my dad. I feel sad w/o you guys. I also feel sad because you are not doing well in school. I feel it's my fault. If I would have been more of a mother to you and not too busy trying to get high, would you be doing better in school.

School is so important. It's important for you to keep your grades up. I also talked about getting you back in my life. I'm not ready yet. I want to have a strong foundation in my recovery before I get you back. That's if you want to be with me. I understand if you don't because I haven't been much of a mother. But I want to try if you let me. I want to be with you and I want you in my life. I don't know if I want to stay here in New York or if I want to come home. I'm scared to come home because I don't want to use drugs.

I hope you give me a chance to be a part of your life. In God's time, if it is His will. I love you soooo much, Jallanna. I want the best for you. But you gotta want the best for you too. Please work hard in school. Apply yourself. And watch the people you think are your friends. Don't let them bring you down like I did. I got into drugs because of my so-called friends. They were not my friends. I miss you and think of you always. I hope to talk to you soon.

Love you 4ever and a day! Mommy

Dec. 9, 2006 12:37 a.m.

I haven't written you in a while. I've talked to you a few times. You're always gone when I call. I can't wait to send you your Christmas gift. $50 in Walmart gift cards. It feels good to be able to give today. I am reading this book called The Red Tent *by Anita Diamant. I got to a part in the book that read "the more a daughter knows the details of her mother's life—without flinching or whining—the stronger the daughter." And I felt compelled to write you and tell you some details* *about my life. I was brought up like you, spoiled in a normal dysfunctional family. I drank at 16, smoked weed and cigarettes at 18, smoked cocaine (crack at 20). Prostituted off and on for 10 years to support my habit. I started doing crack in June or July 1994 after you were born. I lost everything by Dec. 1994. Then I lost myself, self-dignity, self-respect, self- worth, morals, values, then I lost you. I think I lost you B4 I lost self. I don't know. It all happened fast. Drugs ruined your life, my life, and hurt everybody who loved me. Drugs turned me into a person I didn't want to be. I did things I didn't want to do for drugs. I did Anything to get high. I've been raped a few times due to the lifestyle I chose to live. I did a lot of things to people that was wrong. I became a person totally opposite than my mom and dad brought me up to be. I am telling you these things so you don't make the same mistakes I did. Please learn from my mistakes. Drugs ruined our lives. What thing makes you turn against your parents, family, and daughter, your own flesh and blood. DRUGS DO. They changed me and they will change you if you choose to indulge. Please stay away from drugs. Alcohol and weed are drugs also. Don't get it twisted, baby girl. I love you. Miss U every day and I think of you always. My heart aches for you.*

Love,
Mommy

The journaling in my daughter's book helped me tremendously. I did a great deal of writing; it was therapeutic for me. It helped me to process my feelings as well as gauge where I was in my recovery process.

On July 26, 2006, I wrote this letter to say goodbye to my addiction. I still keep this letter attached with a magnet to my refrigerator door. I do not remember why I wrote this letter. It may have been an assignment from my group or I may have written it to sort out my feelings.

I have to admit you really had me. I am writing you this letter to let you know fuck you and goodbye. You are nothing but a liar. I did everything for you. And you always let me down. I thought you were my friend and lover. But you were my enemy. Friends and lovers don't do what you did to me. I did things

I normally wouldn't do. I left my family, turned my back on my daughter for you. I lost myself fucking w/you. I'm talking about my self-esteem, dignity, and self-respect. You were the reason I was lonely because as long as you were around, nobody wanted anything to do with me. Not even me. I wanted to die. You turned me out. I allowed people to violate my body to be with you. You always left me. Where were you when I was standing on the corner at 6 a.m. and and the kids on the school bus would call me crackhead ho. You always made me cry. I thought you were comforting me. Where were you when those men raped me and left me for dead. Where were you when I let those men bounce up and down on me. Where were you. You always left when I thought I needed you. I couldn't feel because of you. I changed into a person I didn't want to be. Well, I'm here to let you know I am letting you go. I take you seriously. You scare me. You are a power greater than me that wants to kill, destroy, and make me suffer. You are a liar and a thief. You have taken everything from me. And I'm not talking about material shit. I'm talking about love f/ others and for self, loved ones, memories, time, which I cannot get back. Dignity. Spirituality. The ability to have choices, 'cuz you gave me none. I need you to know I have choices today. I choose to take my life back. I have found something greater than you and me. He loves me and wants the best for me. He's helping me recover f/ the damage that you've done. He is dependable, trustworthy, forgiving, helpful, and powerful. He is always there. He was there with me and you but I turned my back on Him. He never left me. I left Him. He gave me and others a 12-step program to go to that I participate in. I see you there a lot. He helps me live life on life's terms. He carries me through when I can't handle things. I no longer need to run to you. I choose reality and peace. I know you are waiting for me. But as long as I keep God first and apply my program, you can't touch me. I am not existing or surviving today. I am living. You only exist. I am a part of humanity. I love me and who I am growing to be. As long as I keep working diligently to better myself, you are nothing. I deserve to be loved and to love. I deserve to live. I deserve to be me.

I keep that letter to remind me not to go back. That letter is a power that is greater than me--a gift from my Higher Power. When I start reminiscing and having crazy thoughts about active addiction, I see that letter, and I am restored to sanity. That letter reminds me of what I do not want to return to. It keeps me moving forward. It helps me to continue to live—instead of just existing—and as I live, good things continue to happen.

9

Many lessons to learn

In the summer of 2007, Jallanna came to visit me in Rochester. She was 13 years old. Despite all my phone calls to her, I felt like I didn't know a lot about her. I had not seen her since she was 9 years old! We had celebrated Thanksgiving with my family, and then I disappeared, ending up in Rochester.

I wrote this in my journal the night before Jallanna's arrival.

July 25, 2007 11:30 p.m.

Hey Girl, it's been a long time since I wrote you. Probably because I've been talking to u more. I can't sleep. You are coming tomorrow and I am anxious, excited, and scared. I'm scared because I don't know you. I can't wait. I just got through talking to Paul. You were supposed to be spending the night at his house but you were getting your nails done and it took too long. I miss you soooo much. I am happy I'm going to see you tomorrow. We are going to have fun. I am going to try to get me some sleep. I will see you tomorrow.

381 (this is an acronym for I Love You—3 words, 8 letters and 1 meaning)

Love,

Mommy

July 26, 2007 12:22 p.m.

Day 1, 1st night

Hey, Llannas, I am overwhelmed to see you. I cannot believe you are here. I am happy we have this opportunity to get reacquainted. You're asleep right now. I am almost in tears. I feel intense joy. You are beautiful and special. I thank God you are here with me right now. You are silly. You were licking my hand tonight in the meeting. That tickled. I am overly happy you are here. I love you so much. We had "The Talk" tonight. I showed you how to put a condom on w/ a cucumber. The cucumber was too big but I got it on there. We also talked about sex. I hope you wait a long time to have sex. There are a lot of deadly diseases out there and you can get pregnant. Just wait baby girl. I love you. See you in the morning.

381

Love,

Mommy

During this time, I was still going to the meetings at the Jennifer House, and the counselors helped me prepare for Jallanna's visit. I had everything planned out for us to do. She went to the Spiritus Christi Church's day camp when I was at work. When I wasn't working, I was with her at the day camp. They had lots of activities for the kids. We all went to Rochester Mayor Robert Duffy's office and had lunch with him. That was pretty cool, and the kids really liked that. They met some people who had been homeless and were now living in a house that they were rehabbing. We went to Underground Railroad sites, to Foodlink, to Mt. Hope Cemetery. Until then, I did not know Rochester had so much history. Jallanna and I learned about the city of Rochester together, which was pretty awesome.

On the last day of the camp, we went to Seabreeze Amusement Park and stayed overnight at Father Jim Callan's house, the priest at Spiritus Christi. Jallanna told me, "Mom, Father Jim is cool." He had this big house right smack dab in the 'hood. My apartment was fancier than his.

The house had several rooms, and every room had only a bed and a dresser. He had a twin-sized bed in his room. There was a big table that fit about fifteen people. I have so much respect for him.

This is a man that really walks the word of God. Jallanna really liked Father Jim because he remembered our names.

He said, "Hi, Dellenna. Hi, Jallanna!" And Jallanna and I stared at him. How did he remember our names? Nobody remembers our names, and if they do, they do not pronounce them correctly. Father Jim remembered our names and pronounced them correctly.

I did my best to keep us busy and engaged. We went to movies, watched videos, played Monopoly, and went out for ice cream a lot. Jallanna and I love to play Monopoly; we make up our own rules.

I knew that I had to have a plan for when Jallanna came to visit because I saw women at the Jennifer House getting overwhelmed when their children came to visit after not seeing them in a long time. The kids would stay for about four hours, and the women would get stressed because they didn't know how to be a mom.

Jallanna made friends at the camp. My girlfriends told me if I needed a break, I could bring Jallanna over to their homes. She loves my friends and they love her, too. Having every minute planned out was a bit overwhelming. Trying to get her here and there on time by taking the bus or riding our bikes was stressful. After that, when Jallanna came to visit, I didn't plan anything. We did what we wanted when we wanted. If we wanted to just lay on the couch, that's what we did.

Aug. 4, 2007 12:24 p.m.

You are leaving tomorrow and I don't want you to go. I enjoyed you. I had so much fun. I hope you did, too. We got our eyebrows done this morning. Went to Judy and Terri's and they took us for ice cream. Then we went to the HandI learning day. I took you and Bobesha to McDonald's, then went to movies and saw Hairspray. Went to Jennifer House and hung out w/ Wanda, watched Space Jam and you got sick and threw up as we were leaving. You're asleep now. I had to take some pictures of you while you were asleep because you are beautiful. I love you so much. I am gonna miss being with you. But you will be back and I will come see you. This week went by so fast. You are a beautiful young lady, Jallanna, and I love you. I won't tell I found condoms in your purse. (Smiley face)

If you are having sex and I hope you're not, but if you are, use them. I love you and I will see you in the morning. Love you Big much infinity 2008.

381

Good night.

Love,

Mommy

Before Jallanna arrived, my counselor at the YWCA had me write about how I thought I would be feeling when I dropped my baby off at the airport. I thought I was going to feel sad, weepy, guilty, mournful, heavy-hearted, down, and sorrowful. I learned through that assignment to never project what I may or may not feel. I felt sad to see Jallanna go but also relieved; she was a handful. I was extremely happy and grateful to have had the opportunity to get to know my daughter on a deeper level and thrilled to be able to hold her and look in her eyes. I was overjoyed she came and relieved when she left for Minnesota. She wore me out, and I was tired. I honestly was not ready at that time to be a full-time mother.

After she left, I continued to stay in touch with her and continued to better myself by making goals and accomplishing them.

After I lived at the Y for about a year, I decided to enroll in Monroe Community College (MCC). My sponsor, Kim, was going there, and I knew a lot of people in school. I had to take this test called the Accuplacer to help the college know what classes to place me in. I told people I wanted to study for the test. Everybody kept telling me, "You don't study for it—just go take the test."

Kim, who's a minister, said, "Just go take the damn test!"

"Did you just curse at me, Minister Kim?"

My counselor at the YWCA, of course, was all for me taking the test. I went and took the test, which was not that bad. I had forgotten a lot of information as it had been over a decade since I was in school.

When I went to MCC to sign up for classes, I met with an admissions counselor who asked me a bunch of questions. "What do you want to do?" "What are you good at?" "Where do you see yourself in five years?"

I didn't know the answers. Instead of saying, "I don't know," I started feeling stupid and less than. I was early in recovery and thought, *I don't freakin' know. I go to meetings right now; I'm just learning how to stay clean.*

I started crying. I said, "You know, I don't deserve to be here. I can't do this. I don't need to be here." I remember the look on her face. She didn't know what to do or what to say. I walked out with tears in my eyes.

My disease was telling me, *If she only knew the things that you've done. You don't deserve to be here.*

As I walked out into the atrium, I saw other recovering addicts who were taking classes. I saw one in particular named Lester. I love Lester because he shared about his disability. He's a little slow or mentally challenged. I knew his story and thought, *Wait a minute, he's a slow mother fucker.* I know it's wrong to think that way, but that is honestly what I was thinking. Lester gave me hope that day; his actions both encouraged and motivated me. *If he can do it, I know I can do it. Why should I give up if he didn't?* I later shared with him how he was my hope shot and how seeing him encouraged me to follow through with school. You never know where your help will come from. I do not discount anyone.

After I saw Lester, I turned around and wiped my tears away. I walked back into the admissions counselor's office. She started asking me questions again, and because I was able to say, "I don't know," she knew how to help me. "Well, this is where you're gonna find out, and we're gonna help you find out." She placed me in the basic classes for human services.

For one of my first classes, I was required to keep a journal. Here's my first entry:

Sept. 12, 2007
I am loving being back in school. It's been 14 years since I was in college. I

love it. It is a lot of work, but it will be worth it in the end. I like all my classes. They are in the human services field, math, and English. I have good professors. I also believe I will do well in school as long as I ask for help when needed. I will be at my English professor's door tomorrow to ask for help on my paper. I am happy about doing my field work at JH (Jennifer House). That house has helped me in so many ways. I don't know what I want to do, that's why I chose liberal arts as my major. I know I want to help people help themselves, but I don't know how I want to help. I have experience working with women in recovery because I am a woman in recovery. I want to help other women as well. Well, it's late, I will chat w/you soon.

In my journal, I wrote about my experiences doing field work at the Jennifer House and working for the Healthy Sisters Soup and Bean Works.

Sept. 27, 2007

Today was a long crazy day. I woke up with cramps and PMSing. Had to go to school against my will. Went to pick up a check to get my car out of the shop. Check wasn't ready. I had to be at Jennifer House (field work, 1st day) at 3 p.m.; and it was already after 2 p.m. Finally got check and then I got the car and I made it to JH at 3:05. Still PMSing. I took a client to Walmart pharmacy to get her prescription. I went four aisles over from where she was, came back and she was gone. She was not where she was supposed to be. Twenty minutes later I found her. She went outside to make a phone call. She is on restriction at the house and is restricted from the phone. To make a long story short, she asked me not to tell on her. I told her I wasn't gonna tell because she was gonna tell on herself. Jennifer House has a 10-point system. When you get to 10 points, you have to leave. She already had 9 points. I told her she should have thought about that before she made the phone call. She ended up telling on herself. I don't know the outcome of the situation. It's not my fault if she gets put out. I cannot keep secrets. I feel bad for her. She kept coming up with these excuses for why she did what she did. She could not get honest. Basically, she saw an opportunity to get away w/something and took it. I felt uncomfortable because she reminded me of how I used to be when I was in and out of recovery. I couldn't get honest. I had an excuse for everything. I explained to her how an important part of my recovery is being accountable for my actions (good and bad). I also think about things before I do them. I think about consequences (good and bad) of the choices I make. I do the best I can to be honest with self and that is hard because I tell myself some damn good excuses. I felt I did the right thing today. I don't know how the client feels but I still felt I did the right things.

Sept. 29, 2007

Well, that client at JH (Jennifer House) got discharged. As she was waiting for her ride to come, she was in the bathroom and they searched her purse and found some stolen panties from Walmart. She stole them while she was with me. I feel sorry for her because she is not ready to change. I know because I've been where she is at. All I can do is pray for her. I did and someone saw her in a meeting (12-step meeting), sharing about what happened. So that's a good thing. I had a good day today. I did a tasting for Healthy Sisters soups yesterday at Wegmans. I sampled the Rita's Ragin Cajun and I sold every Rita's soup they had in the store. Today I sampled Spicy Split Pea at Craft Company No. 6. That is a cool store. When I left, they had less than 10 soups left in the entire store. I did so well, Craft Company No. 6 offered me a job. I was flattered, but I had to decline. My plate is very full. I think anybody can sell something they sincerely believe in. Healthy Sisters has helped me. I learned how to be accountable, responsible, committed and show up there. I apply the things I've learned in recovery to other areas of my life, like school, for example. I love my job. The number 1 product at Healthy Sisters is the women's success; the #2 product is the soup. I know I am on the road to success if I keep doing what I'm doing.

Oct. 16, 2007

Today was a good day. I got a lot done. Very productive day. I think I want to change my major if I can. My major is liberal arts. I chose that because I was not sure what I wanted to do. I learned that I love working with the women at JH. I think I want to change my major to liberal arts with human service degree. I like human services. I was not sure before I started school, but I love it now. I love school period. It's hard work but I love it. I am looking forward to choosing my classes for next semester. I'm getting good grades. The drugs didn't take all my brain cells. I am proud of Dellenna. I have a long way to go but I have really come a long way. All I have to do is stay clean and apply myself and I will be ok.

Nov. 19, 2007

I volunteer at Norris Addiction Treatment Center. Every Monday I take the women to an outside 12-step meeting. I did not want to go tonight but I do things on a daily basis I do not want to do. Those things help me stay clean. I did things I did not want to do when I was using, things that were destructive to my life. Today these things I don't want to do are beneficial. I am happy I went because I saw four women I used with. I was happy to see them. They were happy to see me, too. I used to think about them and pray for them. Now they are safe. They can stay safe if they choose to stay clean. I hope they make it but I understand if they don't. Not everyone is ready for the responsibility of change, and it is so much easier to go back to what is familiar – that old destructive lifestyle. I am so grateful I am clean today. I have choices. I have friends, true friends. I am productive and I am loved.

Most of all, I am learning to love myself. I never thought I would be in school and working. I was a hope-to-die dope fiend. I am happy today. Stressed the fuck out with school, 2 jobs, an internship and staying clean, but I am happy. My worst day clean is 10 times better than my best day getting high.

Nov. 25, 2007

I had a nice Thanksgiving. I don't have MY family here but I was not alone. Usually holidays are a bad time for me. But the past 2 years have been beautiful. Thanksgiving is usually a very hard time because Thanksgiving 2003 was the last time I saw my family. I was getting high then. I left Minnesota after that. I am soooo looking forward to Christmas because I will be with my family. I'm a little scared. My mother and father have my daughter and I talked to my mom yesterday and she said she was tired. What she said made me feel guilty. I want my daughter with me but I don't know if I'm ready. I don't want to be selfish and bring her here to New York and take her from everything she knows. I have things here that I started and plan on following thru and finishing what I started. I know my daughter will be more than willing to come with me but I don't think she'll realize the consequences of her choices and what she would be giving up. I just pray to God for help. I believe He will help me. I always say when it's time for me to get my daughter back, God will present the situation and I will be in position to get her. That's a lot of responsibility and I don't know if I'm ready yet. I know my recovery must come first because without that, I don't have shit. I want to do the right thing. And I don't know what the right thing is right now. I do believe and trust that God will help me. I feel fucked up but nobody has ever died from a feeling. It will pass and when the time is right, I will know what to do.

At the end of the class, I turned in my journal to the professor who wrote inside it: *Dellenna, thank you for sharing honestly. You used this journal as I had hoped you would. It's been a pleasure to have you in the class.*

I did really well in my classes at MCC. I chose human services as a major because I wanted to help people help themselves. When I heard talk of the college starting the alcohol chemical dependency degree program, I transferred into that. I thought maybe I could be an addictions counselor. At the time, I wasn't thinking about going on to get my bachelor's degree. I'd completed my field work at the Jennifer House and been hired to be a case manager. I helped the women get food stamps, health care, and personal needs allowance from the county's Department of Human Services. I guided the women and worked with them to develop their schedules for treatment. I helped them to build their self-esteem and found ways to empower them to increase their confidence.

When I chose the alcohol chemical dependency program for my studies, I thought, *I've got the experience of being an addict, so let me get the book knowledge.* People think that because you have the experience, you'll be great at counseling, But no, it's important to have the book knowledge too because you need to know different approaches for counseling different people. What works for one person may not work for another person.

I noticed Wanda's brutally honest approach was totally different than some of the other counselors. Some people in recovery can't handle brutal honesty. I needed to learn approaches to deal with those people too. The academic part taught me how to speak the language, put a label to the things we were already doing. In recovery, we address our thinking and our feelings. By changing the way we think, our behaviors change. I believe my feelings come from my thinking. Every school of thought has a specific language. I was simply learning the language in school, basically naming or putting a label to something I was already doing.

After I had lived at the Y for almost two years, I decided it was time to get my own place. My counselor, Jeanette, told me she was going to retire. The Supportive Living program that I was in was only supposed to be for six months to a year, and I had been allowed to stay a little over two years. Plus, the program had expanded its "no smoking" policy, and we could no longer smoke in the park. We had to go to the sidewalks of Clinton Avenue to smoke, which was a problem. It was safer to smoke in the park. The YWCA also banned cigarettes and lighters in our apartments. I didn't like that. I thought, *Yeah, it's time to be moving on.*

Once my application for the Shelter Plus Care program was approved, I started looking for an apartment. Shelter Plus is a grant program through the federal government where a landlord receives a subsidy on behalf of the renter, and the renter pays thirty percent of her annual income for rent and utilities.

It took me awhile to find an apartment because I didn't want to move into the inner city. The apartments that I saw there that accepted Shelter Plus were not habitable. I was not going to move into a slum or a hole-in-the-wall. With my criminal history, my drug history, my credit history, everything was against me. I was getting a little discouraged trying to find a good place. I did not stay at the YWCA for nearly two years to move right back into the inner city.

I went to an apartment complex in the Rochester suburb of Irondequoit and talked to the manager and her daughter. I viewed an apartment and loved it. When I saw it, I thought, *This is mine.* I knew it. I was so desperate to find housing that I told them everything, my whole story. We were all in the office crying. They wanted to talk to my minister; they wanted to talk to my counselor; they wanted to talk to my sponsor—all these people in my life. I told them, "You can talk to anyone you want to." I thought to myself, *They don't know the apartment is mine,* but I was certain it would be.

The apartment manager and her daughter knew about Section 8 housing (another government housing subsidy), but they didn't know about Shelter Plus. I arranged for my case manager from Shelter Plus to meet with them to answer their questions.

Later the apartment manager called me and said, "You know, Dellenna, we weren't going to let you in. But my daughter called me at one in the morning and said let's give her a chance."

I basically sold myself and Shelter Plus to them, and that opened up opportunities for others. Three of my friends getting Shelter Plus were allowed to move into the complex soon after I did.

When Jallanna was 14, she came to visit me in the summer 2008. I was still living at the Y, and she was with me when I moved into my apartment. At first, we slept on the floor because the only furniture I had was a plant stand, a couple small tables, and a TV. Jallanna and I made a pallet, and we slept right in front of the air conditioner because it was August. About a week later, I got a big couch on Craigslist for $200, and Jallanna and I slept on that.

For that visit with Jallanna, I didn't plan everything like the previous summer. This time, we snuggled up on the couch and watched movies. We played games like Monopoly and SkipBo and Uno. One time we were playing our annual Monopoly game, and Jallanna was cheating. I was cheating, too, but she didn't catch me, and I said, "Jallanna, you're cheating," and we were going back and forth. I threw over the board and said, "I quit! I don't want to play anymore. And pick that shit up!" She looked at me with this surprised look on her face. We both busted out laughing. Now all of our Monopoly games end with the board flipped over and pieces scattered everywhere. I am grateful for the women in my life who taught me that I did not have to have every minute planned. I should just "be with" my daughter.

Here's what I wrote in the journal.

July 27, 2008, 2:26 a.m.

It's been a long time since I wrote you in your book. I think about writing in it, but I never get around to it. You are visiting me now. I am really enjoying your visit. I was a little scared because I don't know how to be a mother to you. I feel sometimes like I am unworthy to be a mother because of the choices I made. I know that is untrue because I am worthy, but I do feel like that sometimes. We had a talk the other night and you told me you were angry, sad and hurt because I kept coming in and out of your life, mostly out. Also, because you don't have a normal family. I needed to hear you say that. I am sorry for the choices I made.

I was very selfish and self-centered. I cannot make up for the past. I missed so much of your life. You are a beautiful young lady. You are a very strong young woman. I admire you. I am blessed to have a daughter like you. I apologize for the things I put you through. You are a survivor. You have so much strength. I love you, Jallanna. I love you so much. I am in heaven when I am with you. I really enjoy your company and getting to know you. You act and laugh just like me. That scares me. I am so happy you are here with me. I cannot wait to get you in my life permanently. I feel whole when you are with me. I will see you when you get up.

381

Mommy

One day, my apartment manager called me and said, "We have a woman who lives in the building next to you, and she's moving. She said you can come over, and whatever you don't take, she's throwing away." I got a whole bedroom set—the dresser, the nightstand, the bed, the TV stand. I also got pots and pans.

I was grateful to this woman, and she was grateful to me because she didn't have to haul her things to the garbage. I could use them. That's how I slowly got my apartment furnished. I saved up my money from working part time at the Jennifer House to buy curtains and other furniture.

My life continued to change and improve. The people and the facilities where I received guidance were a blessing. I allowed them to help me. I am grateful for how they built me up and continued to believe in me when I did not believe in myself.

My time at the Y was incredibly transforming. I moved there early in my recovery, feeling vulnerable, not sure if I could stay clean but wanting to more than anything. When I moved out of the Y, I knew I was ready for more independence, but I continued to stay connected to my foundational supports like the Jennifer House and the YWCA. I could not have foreseen that by continuing to work hard and be focused, and above all—staying clean—that my life would change in ways that I could not allow myself to dream when I was homeless and in the depth of my disease.

10

Helping others in recovery

When I was in prison in Texas, church people came to teach Bible study classes. They gave me a pretty Bible made of thin rice paper with gold edges. One of the teachers was a prophet. She told me, "You're going to be speaking in front of hundreds of people." I was like "Whatever. I'm in jail." I couldn't see that happening.

But the prophesy came to be in 2008 when I gave a speech to hundreds of people at the annual Women's Empowerment luncheon sponsored by the YWCA of Rochester. I stood at the podium on the dais where the dignitaries were seated in a big ballroom. Here's the story I told:

Hello, my name is Dellenna Harper, and I am delighted to be here today. I am delighted to be here because I wanted to share with you just how important the YWCA has been to me. In short, the YWCA helped me to save my life.

I had become heavily addicted to cocaine, turned my back on my family, and lost myself. I hitchhiked all over the country with truck drivers and was on a very steep downward spiral. Finally, when I ended up in jail, the last time, I decided to make a change. I always had good intentions, but without action, good intentions mean nothing.

When I was released, I was sent to a halfway home called Jennifer House. I pretty much arrived on my belly. My stay at Jennifer House lasted for ninety days, and they helped me to begin my journey. I was on my knees when I left there and arrived at the YWCA. And as you can see, because of the guidance and support I received at the YWCA and a lot of hard work, I am now standing firmly on my own feet.

How can a person go from being so numb from drugs and feeling, so hopeless, to having a fulfilling job and living an independent life? Because the YWCA gave me a home and a caring community where if I worked very hard and applied the help that was offered, I would be able to turn my life around.

It wasn't easy, and I wasn't given a free pass. It was actually just the opposite. There were many rules and lots of structure. Much was expected of me every day. I was told a lot of things about myself I didn't want to hear. Many days it seemed easier to just give up—go back to the old life. But the loving and dedicated women working with me were not willing to give up on me and wouldn't let me give up on myself.

My primary counselor, Jeanette, opened my eyes to who I was and who I could become. She let me see that I could ask for help, in fact that I needed to ask for help. The streets make you hard, and you have to be dead to your feelings. Jeanette helped me see that my feelings could not be ignored, but they did not have to rule my life. I learned that I had to "show up" for my life.

Together we made a plan, and I began to see what I needed to do each day to get to where I wanted to be in the future. God and Jeanette would be my guide and hold my hand, but I needed to do the work. When I slipped up, I was called on it. I began to understand that going through difficult times was the only way I could reach a life I would be proud of.

I learned how to follow through on the plans that we made. Not following through and asking for help used to be my weaknesses. Today I can honestly say they are some of my strongest points. Jeanette always told me that I could do it. She told me that I would always have her help and the help of the entire staff when I needed it. They shared their strength with me. They were part of my dream team.

Jennifer House planted the seeds of my recovery. At the YWCA, I received constant watering, endless weeding, and lots and lots of sun that allowed me to grow and thrive in the warm and caring community in which I lived.

Now I am empowered. I have a full-time job as a case manager helping other women see a future for themselves. I have health insurance and a benefit plan. I have my own apartment, and I'm the one who pays the rent each month. And for the first time in my life, I am financially self-sufficient. I can only begin to tell you just how empowering that is. And I am now in my third semester at Monroe Community College majoring in social work and earning straight As. Next step is transferring to a four-year college to get my bachelor's degree.

I have many reasons to be thankful to the YWCA and its fabulous and dedicated staff. Because of the YWCA, I stand here today an empowered woman of integrity, with dignity and self-respect, a productive member of society, and an asset to my community.

Thank you.

During my speech, I felt vulnerable and transparent, but I kept speaking from my heart. I believe that what comes from the heart, touches the heart. I could not stop crying as I exposed my humanness to a room full of strangers. When I finished speaking, everyone in the room stood up. People were applauding and crying, crying with me. I felt so loved and supported, and courageous, too. My heart was glowing. I could hardly believe that woman's prophecy had come true.

In the year 2008 another milestone happened. As part of my twelve-step program, I worked on restitution. I contacted officials in Hennepin County in Minneapolis, Minnesota to take care of a warrant that was issued in 2003 when I didn't appear in court on a prostitution charge. I have never heard of a prostitute getting a ticket for prostitution. Usually the police officer arrests the prostitute and takes her to jail. When the officer wrote me a ticket, I told him, "I'll see you in court, and I'll bring the bagels!" I didn't make it to court though because by then I had left Minneapolis with the truck driver who eventually brought me to Rochester. After contacting the court officials in 2008, the court gave me a year probation with the condition that I do not catch another prostitution charge. I didn't, and I completed the probation in December 2009.

When I was a student at MCC, I learned, sometimes through word of mouth, about programs that could help me with finances.

I got connected with a New York State program that helps people with disabilities. I qualified because of my drug addiction, and they gave me money for books, supplies, and gasoline for commuting to school.

At a program called Recovery Network I learned about credit and budgeting. I figured out a way to pay off my credit. A lot of people, when they get their grants or student loan money say, "I'm going to get high" or "I'm going shopping" or "I'm going to buy a car" and they may not even have a driver's license. My thinking had changed from my days of addiction. I was more centered now and didn't waste that money. In addition to paying off my credit, I paid for courses to get my New York State driver's license.

Eventually I bought my own car for $1,200. It was a '97 purple Ford, and I called it Barney. I didn't think I would qualify for insurance, so I put the insurance in my then-boyfriend's name. One time when I went out of town, he wanted to use my car. I let him, but when he brought it back to me, the tank was on "E" and the car was dirty. The next time I went out of town, I didn't let him use my car, and when I got back there was a nine-page note from him stuck in the car door and my plates were gone.

I had an appointment, so I called a girl friend to take me there. After that, she took me to get car insurance and then to the Department of Motor Vehicles. By noon I had my plates on the car. My boyfriend was in recovery. I went to a twelve-step meeting just so he could see me in my car. "You and your shenanigans are not stopping me because you want to act like a bitch," I told him.

My experience at MCC was amazing; the professors were awesome. I'm still in contact with Diana Robinson, the professor who created the alcohol chemical dependency class.

Diana and I would debate in class. She would say something, and I would challenge her, "I don't know, Diana, can you please explain that?" Diana is a sharp lady, and I loved keeping her on her toes. There were some other addicts in the class. We had some healthy debates.

When I was taking a statistics class, one of my study group friends invited me to a ceremony where she received this real nice medallion. I wanted one, so I asked her what I had to do to get one. She told me I had to graduate with a 4.0 grade point average and be in the top twenty in my class.

The following May, I was one of the first graduates to receive an associate degree in science in addictions counseling; there were three of us. I graduated with a 4.0 and in the top fifteen of my class, so I got one of those real nice medallions, which I gave to my daughter. I was also initiated into the honor society Phi Beta Kappa.

When I first started at MCC, I wasn't thinking beyond getting a degree there. But as I got closer to graduation, Judy (the founder of Jennifer House) asked me, "So what school are you going to next?"

"What do you mean?"

"Well, you can't stop there."

Nazareth College was the only four-year college in the Rochester area that I was familiar with. Spiritus Christi Prison Outreach had its board meetings there, which I had attended a few times. In the spring, when the tulips in the school's colors of purple and yellow are blooming, the campus is beautiful. I also chose to apply to Nazareth because someone told me that I could "never" get in that school. I absolutely love when people tell me, for no logical reason, that I cannot do something. That motivates me.

Diana Robinson wrote a recommendation letter for my application. She told me in her British accent, "You know, Dellenna, I had to put the word 'feisty' in there because I couldn't think of any other word to describe you, and I most certainly wasn't going to lie for you."

"Did you really put 'feisty' in there?"

"You're damn right I did. I think that describes you very well.",

Judy helped me get a scholarship to Nazareth. I also took out loans and continued to get financial assistance from the state. In spring 2010, I had a social work internship at St. Joseph's Neighborhood Center on South Avenue in Rochester. I had met Michael Boucher, a social worker there, when I first came to Rochester and moved into my apartment from Hope House in January 2004. I had been told I could get some furniture from the center, and when I called and told them what I needed, Mike brought me a sofa bed. He and a friend of mine had a hard time getting it up through the narrow staircase to my third-floor studio, but they managed to do it. I knew Mike was a good person from the day I met him. I could tell he was a mover and a shaker; he made things happen.

While working at Jennifer House, I learned about a lot of movers and shakers who were a part of Spiritus Christi, including Mike. I ran into Mike at an event in 2009. I told him that I wanted to do an internship with him when the time came. But at Nazareth in the social work department, the students did not choose their place of internship; the director of field education placed the students. I had done my research, and I knew my placement was going to be difficult because of my history of felonies and drug abuse. I was proactive and shared with the director that I'd like to do my internship at St. Joseph's Neighborhood Center. She politely said to me, "Dellenna, that is not how things work here. We decide the field placements." Long story short, I ended up working with Mike, and I absolutely loved it.

Usually, Mike's interns have to be working on a master's degree, but he allowed me to work with him. I learned a lot about myself during that time. Mike was very encouraging and helped me not only to accept myself but also to embrace Dellenna. He helped me to gain confidence, which I lacked tremendously. He taught me better ways to do what I was already doing. He helped me build on the skills I already had. I learned a lot of "Here's the right way to do something, and this is the even better way to do it."

I learned therapeutic techniques in class and was able to apply them to see how they played out at the center. I worked with a group called Women on the Move. These women were in the same emotional state as women in the early stage of recovery although they weren't former addicts. They were broken. I learned that we all have the same issues even if we're not all struggling with substance abuse. I used the same techniques that I did with women at the Jennifer House but changed up the language. I'm friends with some of those women to this day.

In choosing my major at Nazareth, I knew I wanted to help people help themselves. At first, I didn't know that is what social workers do. That field chose me. It was a perfect fit.

I learned a lot in my classes that I wanted to try out at the Jennifer House; I was working full time there. I'm all about application, because if you know something and you're not applying it, you'll forget it. Why are you even learning it if you're not applying it? At the Jennifer House, I had a big arena, and the women helped me apply what I learned in school. I'd tell them, "This activity is something new I'm trying; let me know what works and what doesn't." They were the best people to ask. They were the experts.

I had worked hard to become a better writer while I was at MCC, and that helped prepare me for the level of writing that was expected at Nazareth where I had to write forty-page papers for class.

At MCC, I could take my paper into the professor before it was due, and they'd look it over and give me feedback. Then I would make changes and bring it back before it was due, and they'd look it over again. I'd make changes and then hand it in. And I'd get a perfect grade. But the professors weren't playing that game at Nazareth.

When I got there, I said to my professors, "What I'm going to need from you…"

"What you're going to need from me?" (Snort.)

"Yes, what I'm going to need from you is when I hand in a paper, I need you to mark it up. I need you to write on my paper—what I need to improve, what needs to be changed. I need you to show me how to write. I need that; that's how I learn."

If my professors handed a paper back with no comments on it, just "A" and "Great job" I would hand it back to them. "I need some feedback on my writing."

I don't like to write but with continued feedback, I became a more effective writer. Diana really helped me with my writing. She and Angelique Stevens, my English teacher, prepared me for undergraduate-level writing.

One time I got a paper back and it was all marked up in red, and I thought I'd failed—but I got an A on it. The professor gave me so much good feedback, I learned a lot and appreciated the guidance.

One time when I met with her, she said, "You express your feelings so well, are you an artist?"

"No, I'm an addict and that's what we do. We talk about our feelings."

"Oh."

Because I was in recovery and had worked the twelve steps, I had a level of self-awareness of my assets and my shortcomings that the other students didn't have. I had an edge up in some ways. Many times in class, I felt "less than" because of the things that I had done; I still showed up every day. My confidence slowly increased, and I got good grades.

Being a student at Nazareth and disclosing who I was and the things I'd done, helped to change the way students thought about addiction, prostitution, and felons. At Nazareth, I focused a lot of my learning on the re-entry of the addict to the community because that was my expertise. I also branched out to work on a group assignment on female genital mutilation. We found a video of a girl going through the process, and I wanted to show it to the class. The other students in my group asked me, "Are you sure you want to do this?"

"Hell, yes! This will bring it home," I told them. I'm big on visuals. It's one thing to just talk about it, but to see it just brings it to a different level. We did warn the class: "If you don't have a strong stomach, you may want to close your eyes." Even though the professor couldn't watch and left the room, she didn't object to the video. "That's what we need to see," she said. We got an A+ on it.

My whole experience at Nazareth was an awakening and a confirmation. The code of ethics of the social work profession confirmed my personal beliefs. I always believe that the people I council are valuable, and they have the right to make their own decisions. My goal is to support them through that. It's not about whether I agree with them or not. This is why Wanda and I used to get into arguments so much. She would try to push her beliefs on me, and I am naturally rebellious. She meant well and she was usually right. I did not like being told what to do.

When counseling a Jennifer House resident, I understood that she is the expert of her situation, and I needed to help her realize that. I had to figure out how I could support her and walk with her because she knew what she needed; she just might not have been able to articulate it yet. I could walk with her and guide her, but she needed to do the work.

I liked that my personal values are aligned with the code of ethics and the values of the Spiritus Christi Prison Ministry Outreach. I truly had found my passion. I think that I was able to bring Jennifer House to another level because of my academic experience.

When I graduated from Nazareth in 2011, my mother, father and Jallanna came from Minnesota, and my boyfriend at the time, Milo, came from California. Like many times with my family, things did not go as smoothly as planned. We spent the night before my graduation at the hospital because my dad's oxygen tank wasn't working properly.

It worked when it was plugged into the car but not when it was plugged into the wall. Before we went to the hospital, we went to an all-night Walmart four times trying to get the right converter or part. I remember we were standing in line at the cashier and we saw this little girl, she had to be about 4 years old, standing in front of us with her mother. We saw her take a piece of candy off the rack and start eating it. She just looked at us and said, "You better not tell!" I'm like *OK, she just stole the candy and she's threatening us.* We didn't tell but I paid for the candy when it was our turn.

While we were at the hospital, my dad finally got a hold of the company in Minnesota where he got the oxygen tank. The guy said to my dad, "Shit happens, Mr. Harper," and my dad said, "Excuse me, shit happens?" I said, "Dad, give me the phone." My family wouldn't give me the phone because they thought I was going to go off on the man. I said, "I'm not going to cuss them out. I'm graduating tomorrow as a social worker; I can handle this." They still did not let me talk to the man.

Eventually I went outside to smoke a cigarette and called the company. I talked to the man who was extremely rude. I did not curse at him, but by the time I got through talking to him, he had told me that his dad was in the hospital. I said, "So you understand where I'm coming from. I'm sorry you are going through this. But now we're both in the same boat, and maybe you shouldn't even be answering the phone for customer service."

His brother called me back and apologized, and they refunded us $300.When my mom and dad went home to Minnesota, the company upgraded their whole oxygen setup at home for free.

We got home from the hospital at eight the next morning, and I had to be at graduation at nine! We didn't get any sleep. That's how it is with my family. They need their own reality show, *Hangin' with the Harpers.*

But everything worked out. My dad cried he was so happy. It was awesome that he could come. At first, he didn't want to come. He had told me, "I'll come to your graduation for your master's." And I said, "Well, Dad, you might not make it there, you might be dead and gone by then, so I would like you to come to this one." He didn't want to be a burden to anyone because of his health issues.

When I walked across the stage to accept my diploma, I heard the words "cum laude" said after my name was announced. I thought, "Why are they speaking Spanish behind my name?" But then I found out it was Latin, and it means "with honors".

Afterward the graduation ceremony, we went to Sticky Lips BBQ, a popular restaurant not far from the Jennifer House. My dad used to smoke meat in a refrigerator that he made into a smoker, but he can't do that anymore because he's on the oxygen. He used to make the best smoked meats: turkey, raccoon, squirrel, goose. All the neighbors loved my dad's barbecue and my mother's cooking; they loved her greens. My dad liked Sticky Lips but said it wasn't as good as his. I'll admit Sticky Lips ain't got nothing on Daddy's barbecue.

When Milo and I took my parents and Jallanna to the airport, everything went south in about five minutes. My mom couldn't find the boarding passes; they had too many carry-ons; my dad was yelling at Jallanna; Jallanna's crying. Like I said, *Reality Show: Hangin' with the Harpers.*

I consolidated bags into bags so they wouldn't have too many. My mom found the boarding passes, and I talked to Jallanna to calm her down. When they all got on the plane, I said to Milo, "I need a drink, so you're going to a twelve-step meeting with me." I went to this meeting called "All in the Family." It used to be my homegroup. I always seem go to that meeting after dealing with my family. I love my family, but they can be so chaotic and dysfunctional at times. I guess it's the typical dysfunctional family.

When I graduated from Nazareth, I was promoted to house manager at the Jennifer House.

But I wasn't finished with college. Although someone had told me that I could not get my license in social work because of my criminal and drug history, my friends encouraged me to do so. I found out that I could obtain my master's degree in two years attending classes part time in an accelerated program. After talking to some people I trusted, I decided it was doable. I knew it was not going to be easy working full time and doing an internship for twenty hours a week, all while keeping my recovery first. I had already been in school for four years. I knew if I stopped or took a semester off, it would be a while before I felt ready to go back. I might never go back. I decided to keep the momentum going and am so grateful I did.

I applied for a graduate degree through the Greater Rochester Collaborative Master of Social Work Program, which is a collaboration between Nazareth and the College at Brockport. But it wasn't easy to get in. I felt dehumanized by the application process. Individuals in the admissions department kept telling me that I had "special circumstances" meaning my criminal record of felonies and prostitution.

I felt like I did the crime, and I did the time, but society wouldn't let me forget about it. I had to fill out a lot of paperwork and the process took longer than normal.

I kept calling the admissions department to inquire about the status of my application. The response was, "You just have to wait because of your special circumstances." I was probably rude, but I would say, "You mean my prostitution and my felonies?" I thought, *Just call it like it is. You guys are trying to be so politically correct.* I laugh about it now.

Fortunately, my professors at Nazareth went to bat for me. I love them. The people that God puts in my life are just awesome. I didn't find out I got accepted into the program until about three days before classes started.

I did the accelerated program part time, going to school for two years, while I worked full time. It was really about time management and sacrifice and discipline. I still went to the twelve-step meetings because I learned early on that I had to keep my recovery first. Recovery is my foundation for everything. Without my recovery, I wouldn't have anything else. I wouldn't have Dellenna, I wouldn't be able to be successful in school, I wouldn't even be who I am or be connected to my family—so recovery comes first. I am clear that if I do not stay clean, I will lose everything and become a derelict once again.

I'd sit in a twelve-step meeting and do my homework. Some people would say, "You know, you're in a meeting, you shouldn't be doing your homework."

I would say, "Fuck you. Mind your business." I tend to speak my mind and it's really raw sometimes. I have learned to filter my thoughts. I have noticed that people watch what I do. They've shared that "I saw you coming here to the meeting and doing your homework and that gave me hope that I could do it." That made me feel good. Now I'm a hope shot for some people who thought just the way I had. *I can't do this. I don't belong.* Hearing from them was comforting to me.

I'd sit in class and sometimes think, *I don't belong—if my professors only knew who I really am, the things I have done. Why didn't I know the answer to this and that question?* But I developed a comeback to those thoughts in my head. *Yes, I do belong because I've earned my seat here. I'm not supposed to know the answers to all the questions. That's why I'm in class—to learn. Who cares about the things I have done? I am not that person today nor am I making those same decisions.*

Every time I thought about quitting, my support network encouraged me, and threatened me, and bullied me. "You're not quitting!" A friend once told me, "If you drop out of school, I am going to drop-kick your ass back into school." She was bigger than me and could be scary at times. So, I didn't drop out.

During my college years I was invited to sit on various boards, which was a boost to my self-confidence. The first board I joined was the Spiritus Christi Prison Outreach Advisory Board while I was attending MCC. At that time, I did not even know what a board was. Judy asked me if I wanted to come to a board meeting. She told me they would have food. I like food and I trusted Judy, so I said "OK!"

I was given a list of all the board members. They were doctors and lawyers, social workers, and mental health therapists—all these prominent people with impressive titles and letters behind their names. Behind my name it said simply "case manager." I thought, *How the hell did I get here with all these people and why am I here?* I never told anyone this, but in the beginning, I felt as though I did not belong—once again.

Early on, I'd sit, listen, observe, and learn.

What really surprised me was that the other board members, with all their titles and degrees, wanted to hear my opinion. They didn't have the first-hand experience of being an addict or being homeless or having a criminal record or working with women in recovery. I learned to speak up when I had something to say.

When I was attending Nazareth, I was invited to join the YWCA Board of Directors. The YWCA board meetings were not as relaxed as the Spiritus board. They followed parliamentary procedure and had many committees I had to participate in. I was happy that I had learned about parliamentary procedure in the twelve-step program along with becoming familiar with the bylaws of a board and guidelines of a committee. That made me feel confident. I later became chair of the Racial Justice Committee of the YWCA for two years. I was comfortable as chair who mainly facilitates the discussion.

I later was approached to participate on the Delphi Drug and Alcohol Board, which was the best learning experience I've had on a board. I learned so much of value while serving on the program and nominating committees and working alongside people with a wealth of information. Some members of that board served as my mentors as well, whether they knew it or not. I felt comfortable utilizing my voice on this board when I had something to say.

Speaking of mentors, Jim Smith, a quiet but powerful and gentle soul, was also my immediate supervisor for many years after Judy retired. He allowed me to intern with him at Spiritus Christi's new housing project called Voter's Block. We were able to provide permanent housing to the people we served at Voter's Block. As I mentioned before, Spiritus is full of "movers and shakers" who make things happen.

At Voter's Block, I worked closely with Jim. Once again, I learned a lot about myself and improved in effectively assisting the people we served. He taught me that it is OK to feel with the people we are working with, to be fully present to them. In doing so I could cry with them and be my genuine and authentic self. He gave me permission to be human with the men and women we served. Mike taught me how to feel with my heart; Jim taught me how to guide and be a leader with my heart.

Although I was learning the skills to be more effective professionally, they helped me in my personal life as well. Not only was my relationship with myself improving, but my relationship with my family, specifically Jallanna, was improving. I was being fully present in her life, listening and feeling with my heart.

In 2012, Jallanna graduated from high school. It was a very proud moment for me and my parents. A few weeks later, on July 5, and back in Rochester, I wrote this in my journal:

Aaaah, I am sitting here. Finished my homework and thinking of you. I was looking at pics of your high school graduation. I'm soooo proud of you. My baby is a young woman. You are growing up to be a beautiful young lady.

I'm sorry Grandpa was tripping on the way to your graduation party. You didn't deserve that on your special day. I enjoyed your party. I wish I could have stayed longer. I watched the fireworks last night, wishing you were with me. The fireworks were nice but I would have enjoyed them even more if you would have been there. I miss you not being here this summer. I really do, but you're growing up. I felt proud to be able to be at your graduation.

I just hate that I missed your prom. You were, you are just BEAUTIFUL. You look like your mamma. I love you and miss you this summer. I also wish you could have been a part of my surprise birthday party. We had fun. You were the only person missing. Love you. I'm going to bed, gotta go to the crazy house tomorrow.

Night,
Mom

In May 2013, I graduated from GRC with my master's degree in social work.

My dad was not able to travel to Rochester due to his health problems, but I was so happy my brother Paul came with my mother and Jallanna. I felt proud. My brother, my daughter, and I drove my mama crazy. We act so silly when we are together.

I had a beautiful graduation party. Everyone whom I love was there, with the exception of my extended family from back home. We laughed, we cried, we ate, we danced. My friends did an awesome job at helping me put the party together. Everything was perfect. Kim even had a little surprise for me. Etch-A-Sketch Comedy crew performed. It was hilarious. My daughter spoke and shared the meaning of her tattoos, which all have something to do with me and our love for each other. I think she used that as an excuse to get a tattoo. My brother spoke about how he was proud of me, and that made me cry. This is the same man who "arrested" me for smoking crack in the church bathroom. Having my mom there was a blessing. I am grateful that they could celebrate with me.

When I graduated with my MSW, Spiritus Christi promoted me to Director of the Jennifer House, the top job. I had worked my way up the ladder. I was proud. On many occasions, my supervisors just threw me to the wolves. I do not mean that in a bad way because that is how I learn. I'd come back leading the pack. I figured things out as I went. My supervisors were open to my making mistakes, and I learned to be open to my mistakes as well. Trust me, I made a lot of mistakes and learned a lot of things the hard way. I remained open, teachable, and always asked for help when I needed it.

Moving up the ladder in the workplace was difficult. I struggled when I began supervising people who were previously my peers. I felt a need to be liked at all times. I did not want to rock the boat, so my supervisory skills sucked, to say the least.

I came to realize that my staff at the Jennifer House was unproductive and unprofessional, and being the leader, I knew I had a part in that. I knew that leading by example sometimes isn't enough. So Spiritus Christi paid for me to take a course with the Ramerman Leadership Group. That really opened my eyes. I realized that nobody at work knew what our vision statement was. So, my staff and I talked about how our personal values aligned with the vision and how we walk them out in our everyday work. We came up with a document—our values statement. Then we wrote our guiding principles and team standards, which were the expectations. The staff came up with this. They were involved in every step so they could take ownership of this process.

We had the staff create their own job titles. This was after I heard one of the staff say, "After all, I'm just 'per diem.' " What she said and how she said it just hit me. We had been calling them the "per diem" and I realized that when you are called something for so long, you internalize it. We gave them each more responsibility, and we gave them titles that reflected what they did. This one is the medical liaison; she's in charge of the prescription medications. The corrections liaison is the link the jails and prisons with the house manager and director.

The staffers who weren't getting with the program either quit or got terminated. I learned that when there's a problem, you just nip it in the bud. I used to sweep it under the rug hoping it would go away. But it never really does. At first, it was difficult for me to just be honest with them.

But Jim Ramerman explained to me, "Dellenna, when you're not being honest with them, you're not being your true self. You've got to be honest with them." I prefer people be honest with me and give me constructive criticism. I learned to say the tough stuff. Before, I was dancing around it, putting pretty bows on it, when I talked to staff. We revamped the performance evaluations, and I learned to say the tough stuff. "If this behavior continues, there's going to be some consequences. And this is what you need to do." Kim stepped up and did the monthly supervisions, which was incredibly effective. I followed through with the performance evaluations three times a year.

In my leadership class, we met three days per month for six months as a group, and then I met with Jim one-on-one once or twice a month. A lot of what we did in the group I was familiar with because of the work I had done in the twelve-step group. I was surprised to find out there are people in powerful positions who struggle with lack of self-confidence or self-esteem. We were able to get vulnerable with each other. Being able to identify with someone who felt the same way I did was comforting. I learned I was not alone.

With my help, my staffers turned themselves around. I know I had something to do with that, but they did the work. I loved being able to brag about them.

The mentors in my life have been a significant impact on my growth—Jim Smith, Judy Simsor, Kim Valentine, Michael Boucher, Diana Robinson, Wanda Johnson, Jo –z Powers, Samone Thomas, just to name a few. I've learned that when you show up and do the work, it really pays off. That's where the courage comes in, like when I was scared to go to MCC. Now I know that any time I experience something new and different, there's going to be a level of discomfort. There's going to be some fear. I know that, and I'm just going to move through it.

The Delphi Board paid for me to go to a leadership board course at 7:30 in the morning at St. John Fisher College. I am not a morning person. At this leadership course, I was the only female, the only black person, and the youngest. A lot of time that's what I deal with. It's not easy. That's when those false beliefs come into my head. *You're not supposed to be here.* But I counter that with *Dammit, yes, you are. These people believe in you and they've invested in you.* It is important for me to surround myself with people who believe in me even when I don't believe in myself—yet.

My life has been such a humbling experience. Everything I have been through was for a reason and serves a purpose. I will never stop sharing about my life as I know my experiences will benefit others. I am so grateful that I allowed God to help me by embracing the people he put in my path. I am not "just" lucky. Nothing in my life was or is a coincidence. God knew what he was doing all along. All I had to do was show up so God could show out in my life. I am so grateful for my new way of life and I will continue to be of service to others as God is not done with me yet.

Epilogue

I'm fourteen years clean, and I'm living life. I'm not barely surviving like I used to be. I'm handling things as they come. We have a saying in the twelve-step program that life shows up when we stop using, but I really believe that life has been going on the entire time. When we put the drugs down, we show up to life. The program gives me tools to deal with life on life's terms. These tools help me not only to improve my relationship with the God of my understanding but also to gain a deeper, more intimate relationship with Dellenna. I have gained self-esteem and confidence, and I know my worth today.

The tools also assist me in quieting the committee members in my head when they are negative. I have a support network of people who believe in me when I don't believe in myself. I'm grateful for the twelve-step program because if it weren't for it and my willingness to do the work, I wouldn't be who I am or where I am. I'm grateful that I am a part of humanity today and not standing on the sideline watching life go by.

I remember standing at six or seven in the morning on Lyle Avenue in Rochester, catching dates and watching people going to work. I'd say to myself, *That's supposed to be me. That's supposed to be me.* Today it is me. I don't always like going to work at 6:30 a.m., but I'm grateful that I'm not standing on the corner.

Thanks to the work I've done in recovery, I have attained the ability to accept personal responsibility by actually moving into the solution of everyday problems. I want all that life has to offer. For me to reap the benefits of life, I have to do the work. I'm OK with that because I've taken from society for so long. I don't have a problem with giving back.

When I moved home to Minnesota, I was scared of the unknown, but I stepped out on faith and God did the rest. Any time I do something new and different, I feel uncomfortable and a little fearful. Although I was fearful, making the decision to move back to Minnesota to help care for my parents also excited me. I saw it as the next part of my journey, the continuance of everything that I've learned in Rochester. I planned to take everything I had learned, spread my wings, and let my light shine. Leaving Rochester on March 6, 2017 marked the next chapter of my life.

What most frightened me was the idea of living near my family and experiencing feelings and situations with them on a closer level. I knew that I'd have to be cautious because it would all be new. Some people say the disease of addiction is a feelings disease, but I believe it's a thinking disease because our feelings come from our thinking, and our disease is the way we think. Addicts have a way of thinking that's not normal.

I moved back knowing I would have to be mindful, aware, and vigilant. I knew it was doable because I'd seen people do it all the time. I just hadn't done it. I recovered in Rochester, and when I visited Minnesota, I was on vacation. This time, I was in it for the long haul. There would be no more going back home to my perfect little life in Rochester where I was familiar with managing my emotions. The spiritual principles of the program are in me. I can go anywhere and recover. Once you practice something for so long, eventually it becomes a part of you. I went from practicing the spiritual principles to living the spiritual principles.

I'm not saying I'm a spiritual guru, but throughout the day I ask for guidance. *Take my will and my life and guide me in recovery and just show me how to live.* The God of my understanding works through people, places, and things. As long as I stay connected and open to guidance and not limit who I allow to help me, I will continue to grow on my journey. I never know who or what God is using to help me.

Since being home in Minnesota, I have continued to build a positive support network of people in my life. It has not been easy. For a long time, I kept comparing people to those I left behind in Rochester. I had built up eleven years of relationships there. I felt like a newcomer all over again, learning who I wanted in my circle, as I am picky. I prefer to have people who challenge me and push me to greatness.

I was excited and scared to be closer to my daughter, Jallanna. I was fully aware that parenting an adult child is different than parenting a young child—to say the least.

Although I did not raise my daughter, when I got clean, I did find creative ways to show up in her life. We called and texted on a regular basis, and she showed me how to connect on Facebook. We built a unique, long-distance relationship. We also looked forward to seeing each other when she came to Rochester for the summer and when I went to Minnesota for Thanksgiving or Christmas. But I did not know what to expect when I moved back to Minnesota where I could be physically present with her at all times.

I knew that I would have a village of people to turn to for assistance, and I am not afraid to ask for help. Children don't come with instructions, right? I have been using the tools of the twelve-step program to help me navigate that relationship.

Since I've been home, our relationship has evolved. She is now in her mid-20s. We have an open and honest dialogue today. I am able to set healthy boundaries with her by sticking to my no's when I really want to say yes. She has to learn from her experiences. I will not rob her of life's valuable lessons by not allowing her to bump her head, especially after I have shared with her my thoughts on a matter. She is going to do what she wants to do anyway. I love her and support her through her decisions, even when they are bad ones.

I try not to parent my daughter out of my feelings of guilt. Thank God, she has forgiven me, and most importantly, I forgave myself. I no longer hold myself hostage for choosing drugs over my daughter and being absent from her life for almost ten years. What I learned is that my family forgave me a long time ago. It was Dellenna who did not forgive Dellenna. I stopped beating my own ass and put the bat down.

Thank God for the program because I do not know what I'd do without it in dealing with my parents. It has been one crisis after another with my mother's dementia progressing and my father's health failing. My family and I moved my mother into a care facility, and I bought a house and moved my father in with me. Caretaking takes a lot of patience, tolerance, understanding, love, willingness, service, prayer, and more love.

My mother is, and has always been, a hoot. With the dementia, things are different. She is still the sweet person she has always been; however, she does not remember her family these days. We are whoever she wants us to be; it's her world. My father is another story. I have to be quick witted with him because he always has something sarcastic to say. He is always talking about "if you see me fighting the bear, you help the bear." I told him I was going to give the bear a straight razor. When I ask him to do something, he says, "If I do, a snaggletooth mosquito will bite me dead in the crack of my ass."

My usual retort is, "What in the ham sandwich are you talking about, Daddy?" A snaggletooth mosquito? My father is a trip.

I could write a book about coming home to take care of my parents. It would start with how I took them to Walmart. After I got them seated on motorized shopping carts, they took off and ditched me. I could not find them anywhere. Then I heard "beep beep beep" and a crash. My father knocked over a display of hats and soon after my mother knocked over a huge display of Honey Nut Cheerios. I could tell that other customers felt bad for me, but I thought it was hilarious. You cannot make that shit up. Another episode of *Hangin' with the Harpers.*

Needless to say, I am very grateful for this time with my parents. It is not easy but it is such a gift. Gifts come in strange packages. I can look at it as a burden or I can look at it as a blessing. I thought I was walking away from my life to take care of my parents, not realizing I was only walking into my life. Life goes around in a full circle. I am truly blessed to have this opportunity to care for them as I had always prayed for my parents to see me clean.

As long as I am still breathing, I will do whatever it takes not to return to active addiction. I will attend twelve-step meetings, work with my sponsor, and do the work to stay clean. I will continue to walk out the spiritual principles that are instilled in me, and in doing so, I will continue to grow into a new and improved Dellenna. After all, it's not where you are that counts—but where you are going.

Acknowledgments

I thank my Heavenly Father, God, for never leaving me and continuing to bless me on my journey in the wilderness.

Jane Sutter Brandt, who guided me through this process, hung in there with me and helped me put a thought into action and eventually manifest a dream that Kim and I had joked about. Thank you for not judging me while I shared my raw truth with you. God could not have sent a better woman to walk with me on this part of my journey. I appreciate your patience and understanding throughout this whole project. You are awesome. I love you.

I will forever be in debt to my Rochester, N.Y. family. Thank you for believing in me when I did not believe in myself and helping me to find a new way to live. The Spiritus Christi Community, the Prison Outreach, and most certainly the Jennifer House, I stand tall and proud on the foundation that you are a part of.

Mom and Dad, I thank you for loving me and instilling in me morals and values. So many times I prayed to God for you both to see me clean, I was not sure if you or I would live long enough to see that day. —I thank you for the last fourteen years of new adventures and making new memories. I am truly blessed to have been gifted the both of you.

My family, Jallanna, Paul, Roxanne, Johnny, and April, thank you for the countless prayers, cheering me on, the continuous encouragement, and loving me through it all.

Damontiz, thank you for sharing your dreams and aspirations

with me. In doing so, you fanned the flame in me. Don't forget about the little people when your time comes.

All my nieces and nephews, thank you for loving me and accepting me just as I am. I know you all think I am crazy—and you are right.

Thank you, Diana G. Robinson, for your honesty and guidance. You truly are a gem in my life.

To my sweetie William Steele, God knew what He was doing when He sent you. I thank you for accepting me and loving me just as I am. I appreciate your whispers of encouragement and calming presence, which by the way annoys me at times because you are calm even when the situation calls for a more heightened reaction. Most of all, I thank you for putting up with me—my moody personalities and my shenanigans, which I forgive myself for (wink). I love you big much. XXXXOOOO

Dellenna Harper

Thank you, Dellenna, for trusting me to help you tell your story. We spent many hours sitting on your couch, laughing and crying as you shared the most intimate details of your life with me, a new friend. God put us together for a reason and I know that by sharing your story, you will be helping countless people who need to give up their addictions or need the strength to stay in recovery. You are also helping their families and friends to understand addiction better and perhaps give them hope.

I also want to thank Sarah Crupi for yet again finding a way to share her design talents on a book project with me. I'm especially grateful for your willingness to learn a new way to navigate the publishing world and always staying enthusiastic and creative.

Laurie Rawlins of Read Line Editing was a tremendous help in fine tuning the manuscript to make it even better. Thank you for the respect and care you showed.

I'd also like to thank Diana G. Robinson and Jill Arnone who read the manuscript in an earlier, rawer form. Your ideas and insights were a tremendous help. Thank you to our reviewers whose comments appear at the beginning of the book. Your endorsements are strong affirmation that *God's Teardrop* is a powerful story. Thank you also to Chris Thomas for his guidance on legal matters.

A big thank you to my family and friends who have heard me talk about Dellenna and her journey for the past several years. Your enthusiasm for reading her story buoyed me.

Finally, a hug and a kiss to my husband, Gary Brandt, for the care he gives to this writer and editor.

Jane Sutter Brandt

About the Authors

Dellenna Harper is a Licensed Master Social Worker whose passion is advocating for and working with formerly incarcerated women who struggle with mental health, substance abuse, trauma, self, etc. This passion was conceived from her own personal issues struggling with addiction, incarceration, and everything else that comes with that lifestyle. Dellenna is currently Director of Hope Harbor and Harvest Hill Programs at The Salvation Army in Minneapolis, Minnesota. She was previously the Director of Spiritus Christi Prison Outreach Jennifer House in Rochester, New York, where she was a resident in 2006. Dellenna is a proud alumna of Monroe Community College (MCC), Nazareth College, and The Greater Rochester Collaborative of SUNY College at Brockport and Nazareth. She was one of the first graduates of the Addictions Counseling Program at MCC. Dellenna was the recipient of the 2013 Jessica Shackelton Maclay Distinguished Alumni Award, presented by the Nazareth College Social Work Department and was also an honoree for the prestigious Rochester Women's Network "W" Award. Dellenna lives in Minneapolis, Minnesota.

Jane Sutter Brandt owns Sutter Communications, which offers a variety of services, including writing, editing, public relations, publishing, and social media. Jane is the author of "Sutter's Sodas Satisfy: A memoir of 90 years of Sutter Drug Co.," about the business founded by her great-grandfather in Burlington, Iowa. Her most recent book is "Beloved Burlington: Featuring businesses you knew and loved." Prior to founding Sutter Communications, Jane was an award-winning journalist with more than thirty years of experience in newspapers, magazines, and websites. She earned bachelor's and master's degrees from the University of Missouri School of Journalism. She is married to Gary Brandt and lives in Rochester, New York.

Book group discussion questions

1. How was Dellenna's faith in God present throughout her journey?
2. Identity is a recurring theme in the book. How is Dellenna's identity shaped at different points in her life?
3. How does racism shape Dellenna's perception of self?
4. Do you think Dellenna would have made different choices had she been white?
5. What are some areas Dellenna has privilege in? What are some areas you have privilege in?
6. Some people say addiction is a disease and others belief it is a choice. What do you think and why?
7. What are your thoughts about the current state of the criminal justice system and its effectiveness dealing with people struggling with addiction? What about people engaging in prostitution?
8. Did reading *God's Teardrop* impact your mood? If yes, how so?
9. Are their lingering questions from the book you still think about?
10. How did the book's title work into the book's contents? If you could give the book a new title, what would it be?
11. What was your favorite part of the book? What was your least favorite?
12. What did you learn from reading about Dellenna's journey?
13. Are there any areas you wish Dellenna had elaborated upon further?
14. What feelings did this book evoke in you?
15. What was your biggest takeaway from reading about Dellenna's experiences?

Thank you for reading *God's Teardrop.* The authors would greatly appreciate it if you would write a short review on Amazon or Goodreads, which will help other readers find the book.

Made in the USA
Las Vegas, NV
11 February 2022

43613792R00115